Broken Together

PIECE BY PIECE

Yaaqov Black

PAGE PUBLISHING, INC.
Conneaut Lake, PA

First originally published by Page Publishing 2021

ISBN 978-1-6624-2522-6 (pbk)
ISBN 978-1-6624-2523-3 (digital)

Printed in the United States of America

I WANTED TO dedicate this book to and thank the Most High for giving me the strength to complete something like this. As a child, I've experienced abandonment, adoption, depression, college, jail, marriage, divorce, and even homelessness. More focused now than ever, overcoming obstacles I would have never thought, at a time in my life, would be possible.

I want to thank my beautiful and loving fiancée and soon-to-be wife Sonya Carroll-Black. You have allowed me to be me (crazy as all outdoors) and love me like I've never been loved before. Thank you, baby. All your support helped me complete this. I love you, Sonja!

My cousin/brother Maurice Law a.k.a. Reece Dogg, you've been there for me at all times. When I didn't even want you to, you had my back anyway. You've been there for a brotha through the good, the bad, and the ugly these last twenty-four years, cuz, doing your thing how you could while working on being a good father and husband. Respect.

Tyrone Lidge a.k.a. Ty. Man, through my most difficult time in life, you had my back when I was down and out. Bro, you let me do me and start all this without ever hindering me and the dreams I've been trying to reach for so long. I owe you for life.

I give honor and praise to my biological mother and father, Reginald Anthony Black and Hope Elizabeth Jefferson, for bring me into this world and allowing the universe to raise me in ways I needed. My mother and uncles, in their childhood, are on the cover of my book. This picture speaks to my concept for the book.

To my adopted parents, Greg Bivens and Catherine Bell, for bringing in a new child while both having your own and loving me in ways I've never knew existed from family, dealing with me after all my mistakes and anger. Man, what I would be if I didn't meet you guys summer 1990.

Chochi, Chelle, and D. Allan (Jeff, Niechelle, and Daniel Law), man, y'all so dope, always have been, always will be. Y'all gave me confidence when I didn't know it. Always positive energy even in fucked-up situations. I love y'all always.

Keisha Walker, Megan Giles, and Robin Arnold, my sisters, beautiful, strong women who have given me examples of what kind of woman a man needs. I love y'all so much.

Trin, Dime, and Reg—Trina Jefferson, Reginald and Diamond Black. Dime, as you can see, is my main character's name. Although this story is fiction, it reminds me of how we and so many children are broken apart helpless. Losing parents matter to us a lot, but losing your siblings means probably more because you spend most of your life with them. So I just wanted y'all to know I love y'all and I'm here no matter what.

Contents

Chapter 1

What Happened?

BEEP, BEEP, BEEP, beep, beep, beep.

I'm fading back to consciousness, slowly breathing, lying here motionless. I open my eyes to focus, see what's going on and where I am. I look up and it's bright. I see a TV above me, I hear machines, people are moving around, and phones are ringing. That can only mean one thing: I'm in a hospital bed. I look up, and sitting in one of the hospital chairs close to the door is a tall, slim, light-skinned gentleman. He's neatly groomed and well-dressed in some creased khakis, a button-up shirt, tie that matched his pants, and some fresh wheat Timberland boots. He stands up quickly, standing about six foot eight or six foot nine, and walks closer, chewing on his toothpick and looking over my hospital chart while I stare at him approaching me.

"Who are you?" I ask.

"My name is Detective Jones. I've come here to check on you and make sure you're okay. Are you okay?"

"Yeah, I'm good. Head hurt a little bit but...wait, Detective? What happened? Did you find my sister?"

In a sudden panic, I quickly adjust my body in an attempt to sit up but is caught off guard by the excruciating pain I feel on my right side, learning that one of my ribs is cracked.

"Goddamn, that shit hurt! What happen to me?" I am moaning in pain as I ask, with no memory of the beating I just took the night before.

Detective.

"They must have cracked you good. Right now, you're at Cleveland General Hospital, and they picked you up last night. When the police found you unconscious outside of the nightclub, they assumed you were drunk until they took a look at you and seen that you were beat up. With it being an assault and or attempted murder case, they called me. The doctors say you suffered a cracked rib, a broken nose, and the back of your head has six stitches."

"Damn, I... I can't really... I can't remember shit right now."

"I looked at your ID. It says that you're from Arizona, with your student ID in Los Angeles. You play for the UCLA ball team, I see. Yeah, I know you. What you're doing here in Ohio and rolling by yo'self to a club? They didn't take anything, so it wasn't a robbery. Man, what did you do? Fuck with one of the girls or piss somebody off?"

"Naw, nothing like that. I'm here looking for my sister. See I ain't seen or heard from in about a little over a year. My mother and father separated us when we were young. We moved from here in Cleveland when I was, like, eleven years old. Me and my mom went to Arizona while her and my father relocated to Raleigh, North Carolina. My sister was eight years old then.

"I went to North Carolina to see how she was doing a few weeks ago, but when I got there, I found out she left. I learned that my father died, and India had moved back here with some friend of hers. She ain't called me and won't respond to none of my messages by phone or any social network. I'm worried something has happened to her.

"I gotta find my sister [*nervous and frantic*]." I asked the detective, "Can you help me?"

"I can help you. I'll do what I can for now, but you will have to get better first. The doctors say you have a few more days in here to heal. What is your sister's full name?"

"Her name is India Rochelle Williams. She should be nineteen years old now. She just had a birthday two weeks ago."

Detective Jones walks over to Diamond's bedside, reaches in his coat, and pulls out a card.

"Here's my card. I'll do some investigating when I get back to the station. I'll let you know what I can find, but when you're better, call me. We can take it from there.

"You just get some rest. You're going to need the energy, and I'll be back."

"Okay, and as soon as I'm better, I'm coming to see you."

The detective walks over to shake my hand, confirming his obligation to help, nods his head, steps back, and opens the hospital room door to exit. While feeling helpless in my hospital bed, I buzz the nurse to see if she can help me find a phone so I can contact my mother back in Scottsdale, Arizona, to let her know what is going on.

"Nurse, nurse!"

"Yes, sir. How can I help you?"

"Did they find my phone with my clothes? I need to call my mother."

"Let me check for you, sweetie. I'll be right back, okay?"

Confined to my hospital bed now being back in Ohio, I take a moment to reminisce about how great my childhood was here back then and, in an instant, how everything changed and went wrong. In deep thought, I find myself confused, alone, awake in pain, and worried about India.

Chapter 2

The Beginning

EVER SINCE I can remember, India and I never went without anything—presents on Christmas, birthday parties, video games, gadgets, toys, and all the newest and freshest clothes we ever wanted. We received the best education from home and school because our parents both graduated college, had great careers, and led by example in business and in their personal lives.

My father, Professor Emmanuel Williams, was a tall, dark, and fit brotha who was educated, warmhearted, fair, and extremely charming. He taught English Comp I and II at Cleveland State University for about seven years. Dad was very social. He would speak to anyone he would come in contact with. He was well respected and also loved by everyone in the CSU faculty. He inspired and was also admired by any student who took his course, no matter their gender, ethnicity, and/or culture. Sometimes, through his confidence, style, and demeanor, he would find himself with no intentions seducing the eager and always-willing-to-teach female students he lectured.

My mother, Evelyn Meyers-Williams, was a high yellow exotic-looking sista with long straight brown hair. She was aggressive, witty, by the book, and about her business. Not to brag or anything, but she is one of the best leading real estate agents for REMAX Realty in the Northeastern Ohio area. She sells properties faster than most of her colleagues, even her arrogant, privileged male coworkers, who hated that they were outshined by a black woman. She was raised by my grandparents, Sherman and Hope Meyers, who were of the bloodline of the First Nation Indians, so "yeah, we had Indian in our family," as most of us like to say, especially when it comes to our hair, but whatever.

Mom grew up in a middle-upper-class lifestyle in Shaker Heights, with both of her parents and her two sisters Debbie and Audrey. They were brought up balanced by Grandma Hope and Grandpa Sherman with integrity, morals, education, spirituality, rules, fun, discipline, and love. Dad was an only child. He was adopted and raised by his father's younger brother Andrew Williams, my rich and hustling great-uncle Drew. My dad's mom, Debra Carroll, died from drug overdose, and his father was killed in prison before he was ten years old. So Dad grew up learning the game early as an only child. My uncle Drew, in spite of that, always made sure my father advanced in his academics so he can sustain his success in life.

My mother was always there for us at the drop of a hat whenever we needed anything. Nothing was ever too much for her babies, and she made sure we knew that by her display of love, attention, and affection. Dad on the other hand was there but sometimes found himself caught up in work and was too busy to respond to our calls, texts, and even emails.

India, my little sister, was born with a serious case of asthma, so in her younger years, we all took extra care and responsibility for her every day to make sure she received the right treatments needed to maintain her health. As she grew older, her body continued to go through so many changes with this sickness but getting better every year with different forms of cannabis treatments. Dad would always try to keep his time and energy available when it came to India because she was daddy's girl in every way since the day she was born. When we both started going to school, I took it upon myself to make sure India, I, her teacher, and the office had all the medicine, phone numbers, and proper procedures needed to know in case of any emergencies with her health.

Mom or Dad would drop us off and picked us up every day from school, but because they worked so much during the beginning of the year, sometimes they would allow us to walk home together if they were running late. They were nervous and skeptical at first about us walking home alone, but I convinced them I was responsible and old enough to handle it. We really only lived a couple of blocks down the street from our school, so after a couple of times doing this safely, they were okay with it, and even sometimes, it helped them.

Chapter 3

India's Health

ON A WEDNESDAY afternoon in the spring of March 2003, the clock was taking its good old time ending my long and average day of school in Mrs. Wilcox's sixth grade class. I was waiting for Dad to pick us up and take us to McDonald's for a Happy Meal. He made it a habit of doing so every day after school because he knew we were always hungry by 3:00 p.m., and we definitely looked forward to it also. After getting our food, we would head to the house, finish our homework, then later watch our favorite Disney Channel show, *That's So Raven*. When the bell rang that day, I rushed to the hallway in excitement, almost tasting those hot, golden-brown McDonald's french fries I had been craving since I tried to eat that horrible meatloaf, mashed potatoes, and mushy mixed vegetables they served at lunch today. I rushed to my locker to grab my coat and books needed for homework to put in my bag, then I headed to meet India in her fourth grade class on the first floor.

"You can find me in the club, bottle full of bud. I'm into having sex. I ain't into selling…"

I was singing and rapping to myself walking down the hallway to 50 Cent's new hit single "In the Club" while passing the second grade babies walk out of class. I quickly lowered my volume so none of them could hear me recite those not-so-positive lyrics I felt so passionate about. As I approached India's classroom door, I knocked to say hello to her teacher, Mrs. Bennett.

"Good afternoon, Mrs. Bennett. How are you doing today?"

"Hello, Diamond, I'm doing pretty well. How was your day today?"

"It was okay. We are learning linear equations now, and it's pretty cool. I'm just trying to get a hang of it."

"Well, that's good. Let me know if you need any help. Math is my favorite subject."

"I will. Hey, sis, you ready?"

"Hey, Dime!" Without zipping her coat up all the way, she ran over, excited to see and hug me, her big brother.

"Y'all have fun today?"

"Yeah, I did. We had a spelling bee, and I won with the word *phobia*, p-h-o-b-i-a, *phobia*. We did some multiplication too."

"Go 'head, Indi. That's real good! You ready 'cause Daddy's on his way to pick us up. Come on. Let's go meet him outside."

"Okay."

I helped India zip up her coat and grabbed her bag, walked out of Mrs. Bennett's classroom, and headed down the hall to the front entrance of the school where Dad was usually parked, waiting for us. Before reaching the door to exit, I was called out by Mrs. Wilcox.

"Diamond! Diamond! Come here for a minute. I have to talk to you."

In a rush to get out the door, I replied to her, "My father should be outside, Mrs. Wilcox. We have to go."

"That's just it, sweetie. Your father is going to be late getting off work, and he called the office to tell you two to go on and walk home today. He says that he will pick up your McDonald's on his way, so you two can start on your homework first."

Disappointed by the news, I paused, nodded my head to let Mrs. Wilcox know I understand, then I stopped to assure India and I were bundled up before making our rare walk home.

"Hey, sis, Daddy's not picking us up today, so we gotta walk home, okay?"

"Okay, Dime," she said so nonchalantly, grabbing my hand to wait for me to open the door to walk outside.

Not cold but not really warm that day. We started on our way, reaching the corner where the crossing guard, Mrs. Beverly, stopped us while she was patrolling the cars and buses picking up the rest of the students attending Bryden Elementary school.

"Hey, kids, how was y'all day at school today?"

I answered, "It was okay. Lunch today, it was nasty, so I'm still hungry."

India said, "Our dad's gonna pick us up some food when we finish our homework."

I said, "I hope he bring it before we done."

"That's good. I'm glad y'all had a good day. Oh, okay, well, y'all be careful getting home. Go 'head and cross."

I said, "We will. Bye."

Just four blocks away from home, we crossed the street as Mrs. Beverly walked out with us to hold off traffic. While walking, we sang cartoon intros and some toy commercials, enjoying each other's company, skipping along like some happy children down the sidewalk on our way home. Two blocks from the house, crossing the next street, laughing and playing, all of a sudden, India paused for a moment, short on breath. With her face turning blue and a weary look in her eyes, she mustered up enough energy to say one last thing before collapsing—"Dime, help me!"

"What's wrong, sis? You okay? India! India!"

I panicked! Cold chills stabbed right through my spine, freezing my soul. At a loss for words, looking down at my little sister unconscious lying there in the middle the street, I immediately yelled for someone, anybody.

"Somebody, help me!"

Before getting a chance to console her, a silver Ford Explorer came rushing around the corner toward us, trying to beat a light. I reacted as quickly as I could and grabbed India, still unconscious, to throw her out of harm's way. Still in range of this SUV coming toward me, I then braced myself as the mother of three boys heading to football practice did her best to try and stop. Just my luck though, their speed had accelerated too high, so I closed my eyes to think about my sister. The vehicle made contact with me anyway. The moment I was struck, everything went black, sending me twenty feet farther down the middle of the street before it came to a complete stop. I dislocated my left shoulder, broke four ribs, and had a concussion from the impact of my head hitting the ground.

I woke up a day later in this very hospital with Mom and India standing over, watching me. Unaware of what happened, I regained my consciousness, feeling pain all over my body that I had never felt before. I looked up to my mom and sister.

"Hey, Momma."

"Hey, baby! You're awake now. How you feeling?"

I was in a hospital bed dealing with my own pain when Mom asked, and even though she was standing in front of me, my main concern was if my little sister was going to be okay.

"I'm fine, I guess. My ribs and my shoulder hurt, but I'm good. Hey, sis. Momma, how she doing?"

With tears in her eyes, she rushed over and gave me a hug. "Hey, Dime, I'm sorry I passed out, and you got hurt. I promise I won't do it again."

"It's okay. You scared me, and I didn't want anything to happen to you, so I did what I could to help. I just got hurt too."

With tears in her eyes, still shaking but smiling, Mom walked over to my hospital bed and reached down to kiss me on my forehead. In a split second, Momma's mood changed from fear to anger at my father.

"I don't know what I would have done if something would have happened to either one of you. I love you two so much. You were so brave for being there for your sister like that, Diamond. I am very proud of you. If your father wasn't working so damn late all the time at that school, he would have been able to come and pick you guys up, and none of this would have ever happened."

Feeling awkward by her words and with a sudden taste for McDonald's french fries, I thought to change the subject and ask if they could go and get me some McDonald's instead of this not-so-tasty hospital food they was trying to feed me.

"Mom, where is Dad?" Can you tell him, or can you go and get me a cheeseburger Happy Meal? Please."

"I'll go and get it for you. What kind of drink do you want?"

"Orange," I replied, smiling and happy.

"Your father is still at work, but he will be here shortly, I think, to see you. Come on, India baby. Let's go and get your brother something to eat."

I was feeling a little better as I lay here in pain, knowing I was about to get some of those golden-brown fries I had thought about since I left school yesterday. I watched Mom and India walk out of the room, who, soon as they hit the hall, were greeted by my dad, who had just arrived from work with fries and Happy Meal already in hand. *Great for me*, I thought, cheesing, slowly sitting up, preparing to feast on my meal, anxiously expecting for him and Mom to say a few things to each other momentarily, and then he came in. He handed me my food and asked about how I was feeling and all that. But as I looked closer, Mom, for some reason, was angry when Dad came in. She immediately started yelling and cursing instantly, alarming everyone around us, creating a scene and scaring India. I couldn't hear anything clearly because Mom closed the door behind them, but as I observed her movements and expressions in panic, I watched a woman whom, all my life, I saw so loving, secure, outspoken, and strong now crying, broken down, and vulnerable.

Eyes full of tears, she said a few more things to him, then kneeled down to hug and kiss India. She stood up to look at me through my hospital bed door, watching her lips, with a tear in my eye and a sore in my throat, say I love you. She pushed my dad to the side and stormed out of the hospital. Dad tried to chase her down but quickly rushed to tend to India as she cried out for Momma, who was running down the end of the hallway to the stairs. I couldn't breathe, I was scared, and I didn't understand what was going on after all I had just gone through. My heart was heavy, and my ribs were literally broken. My sister was sick, and I didn't know what just happened. *I...am...lost!*

Chapter 4

Mom's Concerns

9:17 A.M., THURSDAY morning, Western time, Scottsdale, Arizona. I'm in my office, always dressed for success—Evelyn Meyers, head real estate agent for REMAX Realty with my MBA and BS. I'm relaxing, just sitting at her desk in front of the computer, searching available properties online, completing some paperwork needed for a property I just sold a few days ago. Focused and into my search and sipping my large cup of coffee that Diamond and India gave me for Christmas 2002 that read World's #1 Mom. I hear the phone ring while I'm trying to concentrate on filling out the last of the signatures needed on a page in front of me. I let it ring a few more times than usual before reaching to grab it, offset by the Cleveland area code I see on the ID. I pause for a minute and then pick up the phone to answer.

"REMAX Realty, this is Evelyn speaking."

"Mom."

"Diamond, hey, baby, what's going on?"

"I'm in the hospital, Ma."

"In the hospital? Was it at practice? What, you hurt? And why are you calling me from a Cleveland area code?"

"I came to Ohio, trying to find India."

"How the hell you gonna go to Ohio and not tell me? Boy, you know you supposed to be in school trying to get better practicing

18

with the team so y'all can at least make the final four next year. We could have gone to see her together."

Upset by my passion for basketball and not his well-being or my daughter's whereabouts, Diamond quickly responds, doing his best not to snap on me.

"Look! I just found out she don't live with Pops no more in North Carolina, and I ain't heard nothing from her in months. You don't seem to care, so I'm taking a break from basketball right now to make sure my little sister is all right. I already talked it over with coach. He okay with it."

"What the hell is going on with your father? How could she not be living with him anymore to be in Cleveland, again. Diamond, why are you in the hospital then?"

"I got jumped by some guys the other night, trying to find her at the strip club down here."

Immediately angered and pissed by his answer, I stand up out of my seat and, in a rage, yell at Diamond, "THE STRIP CLUB! WHAT THE FUCK IS MY BABY DOING AT A STRIP CLUB?"

Anxious to respond in pain and short on patience, Diamond interrupts me to let me know what's going on.

"POPS DIED, OKAY? And from what I'm hearing, India has a friend she met in North Carolina named Delilah that she followed back here to Ohio. I came to find out what's going on, and I don't care if you approve of it or not. I can't focus on school until I know if she okay."

Caught off guard with the information I just received about my children's father, my ex-husband, and at a time, the love of her life, I stop to take a deep breath and sigh before responding back to Diamond.

"Are you okay, Diamond?"

"I'm all right. I'm just waiting to heal some, and then I can go and talk to the detective that came in my room to investigate the guys that jump me. I don't want you to worry too much, Ma. I'll keep you posted as much as I can."

"Boy, you sound foolish! How you gone just up and leave and not tell me? Look, I know you're grown now and able to make decision on your own, but you should have at least talked to me about it. We could have set you up with somewhere to stay, and some of your family there could have looked out for you. Your Auntie Debbie stays in Garfield Heights. I'ma give her your number so she can come and check on you. I can't believe my baby is just out there and haven't called and let us know nothing. What was your father doing for her to be in this position? You find her, Diamond, for us, okay? You find my baby. I got to get back to work, but I might take some days off so I can come out there too. You need some money or anything?"

"Naw, I'm good, I'll let you know if I need something else though. I'm about to get some sleep. I love you, Ma, and I'll keep you posted."

"Okay, baby, I love you. Bye."

"Bye."

Diamond hangs up the hospital phone and grabs the remote sitting on the stand next to his hospital bed. He turns on the TV and gradually falls to sleep to the sounds of Cartoon Network.

Now unable to focus on my work, I hang up the phone, flop down in my seat, and take another deep breath, then exhale with a loud sigh. Emotional, I unbutton my jacket and grab a napkin out of the box placed next to a picture of her Diamond and India in the last picture they took back in 2012. I take a moment to collect my thoughts and then start to cry. Feelings of pain and regret as a mother and nurturer on how much the children's lives have changed, broken apart. Something I never want. Feeling uncertain about the situation, I decide to take the day off and get ready to make my way back East, Midwest, that is. I pick up my phone and let my assistant know. Phone rings.

"Yes, Mrs. Meyers?"

"Hey, Kristi, I need you to cancel my appointments for the week. I have some personal issues I need to tend to back home. You can take the rest of today and tomorrow off. Okay?"

"Thank you. I appreciate it, Mrs. Meyers, I'll take care of those appointments right away. Have a safe trip."

"I will, and thank you. Enjoy your weekend."

* * *

Mind racing now about my family and the events that led us to this situation, I shut off my computer, get up, and grab my coat, then walk out of the office. In a rush out the door, I reach in my purse to grab my keys while slightly jogging, hitting the unlock button, quickly making my way inside to start the car. My phone starts ringing while I put the vehicle in motion. Now heading out of the parking lot, I hit the car's Bluetooth device to answer. It's my current husband, Troy Dickerson. I met Troy the first year Diamond and I moved here and got married three years after Emmanuel and I filed our divorce papers.

Troy is a well-established businessman in his late forties, not that tall but not short about five foot nine. He has a dark-brown complexion with a stocky build. He is real clean-cut, always in a three-piece suit, and a Cuban in his hand. Troy always talks business, has money, and wants everyone to know he does. He has two sons, one each with his first two wives, only being married a total of six years between the two. Troy's two sons—Troy Jr., twenty-seven, and Reggie, twenty-four years old—both still stay back home in Phoenix. Troy is originally from Phoenix, Arizona, but he bought many properties and small businesses around town here in Scottsdale. He is a respected, well-known guy from one of the few wealthy black families in the West Coast. It's been said around town that his great-great-grandfather and uncles killed and stole money from some bank robbers in the late 1800s. They ended up buying their freedom and a large amount of land that helped them build fortunes.

He and I got closer and closer while purchasing a house I sold him years back. After buying his fourth property from me, he moved from Phoenix to Scottsdale to charm and buy his way into my and Diamond's life. I got lonely and needed somebody, so I did what I felt was best for us.

Button click answers.

"Hey, I was just about to call you."

Troy replies, "What's going on? Everything all right? I just called your office, and Kristi told me you had just stepped out for the day."

"Yeah, I gotta take a few days off and go to Cleveland to check on Diamond."

"Cleveland? Why is he in Cleveland? I thought he was in school in LA?"

"He was supposed to be, but my baby India is missing. She is not living with her father anymore in North Carolina. We just found out he passed away some time ago."

"Aye, I'm sorry to hear that."

"I appreciate that. Yeah, Diamond said she is somewhere back home in Ohio, so I got to go and check on my babies. I'm on my way home, sweetie, to book my flight and get packed. Can you meet me at the house?"

"Ah yeah, give me about an hour. I'm about to finish up this meeting with some business partners, but I'll be on my way right after."

"Okay, I'll be there waiting on you."

"All right, just know that I'm here to get through this with you. I love you."

"I love you too, and thank you for being so supportive, Troy."

"Hey, that's what I'm here for. Do you need me to bring you anything?"

"I could take some Chinese food? Lo mein, spicy."

"You got it. Just let me put a rush on this, and I'll see you soon."

"That's fine. I'll be at home."

"Okay, later."

"Bye."

I hang up the phone in the route home. I am feeling very appreciative for Troy who loves and supports me and Diamond with the best, but at the same time, I'm hurting inside, full of every emotion, thinking of Emmanuel who is now dead and gone. Never getting to see him again disturbs me most because in spite of how the relationship ended, I loved him, grew with him, and was very much in love with that man. I wanted to have at least one more conversation with him to talk about why. We were happy and in love, and I never thought I could live without him. Until that day in 2003.

With tears rolling down my face thinking of him, India's whereabouts, and now knowing how much their separations affected Diamond, I reminisce back to that day that changed our lives forever.

Chapter 5

How Could He (Evelyn)

MARCH 18, 2003, 12:30 p.m. I was on my way out of statistics class, exhausted yet excited that I was so close to finishing up the semester to receive my master's degree in business. I wanted to surprise my husband with lunch and a quickie before he taught his next class at 1:30 and then head to pick up the kids later after class. I owed so much of my success to this man; he was the reason that I was elevating myself for our family. Even after two beautiful children, I still managed to keep myself looking flawless and better than most women. I worked out four days a week, stomach flat, skin smooth, hair sharp, ass fat and firm, and my top half that needed no more attention. I was five foot seven, 150 pounds; measurements were 38-26-40, baby, thirty years young, and phenomenal. These college girls ain't got anything on me.

I had to be honest with myself though; I did know men, and I knew my husband could be and was tempted often. So as a woman and his wife, I had to keep him fed sexually all the time and in every spontaneous way. (I had attended a few of his lectures in the past and witnessed his persuasion when speaking to his students.) All these young and innocent girls. He lectured them with this passion and energy but with no intention, instantly seducing them almost defenseless. Standing six foot three, 215 pounds with a firm and demanding demeanor, Emmanuel Williams was a natural ladies' man, and being so nice, he would get a lot of them young girls asking for more personal help to study and to see Mandingo. I couldn't blame them because he had it, and I couldn't get enough of it, so I knew I had to be on my shit and do my best to keep him loyal to me. They were not gonna let up, and I was talking about the women in the faculty too.

I gathered my books, walked out of the classroom to leave the College of Business Department in the Mone Ahuja Building where most of my last courses needed to graduate were taken. I headed to the library and tried to call Emmanuel first to let him know I was on my way but got a voice mail, so I left him a message. With the English department being in the Rhodes Tower and it being the library made it even more convenient because I could study a little bit also. I knew he was in between classes, so I figured he would be okay if we hung out a little before I went back to work and he started his next class, but I kept getting his voice mail. I was going anyway, stomach growling, hungry in more ways than one, but I felt I could wait after we sweat it out on top of his desk to create even more of an appetite to eat some food afterward. I made my way inside the library, passing students on computers, at tables studying alone or in groups and some standing in line, getting coffee at the always busy coffee shop we had inside.

I made my way to the elevator to the eighteenth floor to surprise, seduce, and stimulate my fine-ass husband. I got in the elevator with a few young white girls who brought their conversation they carried through the library in with them. I smiled and greeted them as they carried on, then I stood next to the buttons, awaiting my exit to see Emmanuel. Party, drinking, a wild night were all I really heard from the two young ladies' conversation. In a rush to escape and ignore the college life stories, I looked at my phone to see if he called me back, but no call. I made an attempt to call him again, but no answer. Maybe it was the elevator. Bell rang, door opened, eighteenth floor, finally I was here now; unfortunately, I was not alone as I let the party girls walk out ahead of me, heading, it seemed, in the same direction to the English offices. Impatiently waiting and in need to get to Manny's office *(that was what I called him when I wanted him),*

I walked behind the two girls, slowly feeling myself getting wetter and ready to fill my husband's ten inches deep inside of me. They arrived at the door a few steps ahead but held it open for me as we all entered the office. The two walked up and greeted Travis, the administrative assistant sitting at the front desk, to let him know they were here to see their instructor.

"Hello, how can I help you?"

One of the girls said, "We both have appointments to talk to Professor Clark."

"Okay, sign in right here and go on back down that hallway there."

The two girls stood by to sign and go speak to their professor. Standing behind them, I made eye contact with Travis, who knew me, to let him know I was here to see my husband.

"Hey, Trav, I'm here to see Manny.

"Okay, but…"

I was in a rush, so I never even waited to hear a response from him as I continued heading toward Manny's office. It wasn't cold that day, so I dressed casual in one of my business skirt suits, horny and ready for passion. When I saw him, all I was gonna have to do was lift my skirt up, pull my panties to the side, and let him stroke my wet, warm, and waiting walls of ecstasy. As I walked closer to his door, I saw that it was closed but not shut all the way, giving me a side view of a young lady whom I assumed was a student by first glance. She was gorgeous, very exotic looking, somewhere South America. She had long curly hair with her legs crossed, sitting on the desk facing him, speaking to my husband as if she was upset. A little upset by her feisty tone, I stepped back out of sight and paused to listen in on their conversation a bit.

(*Strong accent*) "Why won't you just tell her? She's gonna find out sooner or later, so you should just tell her now, Emmanuel."

"You know I can't do that. It's not that easy. Yes, I have been telling you I'm going to. I just can't find the time at this point. Please, I just need you to give me a little more time."

"You keep saying that. 'Just give you more time.' You promised, and you know I can't do this alone. I've been waiting for you, but I won't wait too much longer."

"I can't just up and leave my family like that right now! Why can't you understand that?"

"You told me you love me, and now I can't leave you, and I wouldn't feel right if *they* didn't know. So if you don't tell her, I will."

"I promise I will tell her. Look, Isabella, you know I love you. For the sake of my daughter, just give me a little more time, please."

Not sure about his answer and how long she would wait for him, Isabella got up in silence and walked over to look out of the window, feeling uncertain and still angry. Emmanuel got up out of his seat, following her, turned her around to face him, and pulled her close. He grabbed her hands, looking directly into her eyes, hugged and consoled her, followed by a long and passionate kiss, making a promise that they would be together soon.

I, his wife of eight years, the woman who was there through all his struggles, his highs and his lows and witnessed all this shocking information like this. This was crazy, and by faith, I walked in on it! Confirming any doubts, any hearsay, no phone numbers, and no lipstick on the collar. I honestly wasn't prepared for this at all today. You could have told me anything fucked about that would happen to me that day, and I promise you that this would not have been one I could have thought of, I swear. I took a moment to think about my babies and about my job and my responsibilities. I then realized, I needed to check myself and clear my head first in spite of this pain. Because I might just go way the fuck off and catch a case in this *bitch*!

I then exhaled before I turned around quietly and made my way out of the English office hallway without being seen or heard by Emmanuel and Isabel, his new, younger, exotic, student girlfriend. Doing everything to keep myself together, I hurried as fast as I could pass the administrative desk unnoticed, but Travis, giving such great customer service, saw me smirking and said goodbye anyway. I gave him a quick wave back while I walked out the office holding back a face full of tears, headed to the elevator.

I left the Mone Ahuja building, too angry to even try and study anything to stay at the library, so I made my way across campus to my car. Feeling full of every emotion and deeply brokenhearted, I got in the car, closed the door, and just broke down. Too mad and shocked to vent to anyone about this, I just cried, constantly asking myself what I could have done wrong, knowing that even with my education, even with my beautiful children, my loyalty, cooking, cleaning, and sexing, my man daily whom I thought was faithful. He still gave another woman his heart under my nose this whole time so easy. I saw no signs of this. I thought I was doing everything right, but I guess not. I guess not.

At a loss for words I didn't want to do anything else but break something or hurt someone. I knew I couldn't just do nothing or something I may regret later, so instead of soaking in my own tears all day over what Emmanuel was doing, I decided to go and work out. I needed to release some of this rage and tension that were built up inside of me right now. I always packed extra clothes, so I should be good and focused when I headed back to work today. I was also upset that I was burning a sweat this way and not the way I intended. I felt I had to control this situation and not overreact too fast. It hurt like hell, but I had to be strong, especially for India. My daughter and soon-to-be woman, whom I prayed in her future relationships never would have to experience a man's wrath by loving him like this. She would be strong though, inspiring all of us, fighting asthma every day. So yeah, let me work out and clear my head and handle this later. I looked in the mirror and wiped my face, clearing all signs of crying. I repeated a few times to myself one of the many affirmations I learned in a book I read a few years ago. The affirmations were to help you find you when you felt like you'd lost your way or control of your life. They had always helped me, so I continued to keep them in handy when needed.

"You are a phenomenal woman. Your endless good now comes in endless ways."

"You are a phenomenal woman. Your endless good now comes in endless ways."

"You are a phenomenal woman. Your endless good now comes in endless ways."

I stepped out of the car, popped open my trunk, and grabbed my bag. I walked in the direction toward the recreation center. Today, I thought I would run for forty-five minutes, walk for fifteen minutes, lift for thirty minutes, and punch a punching bag for thirty minutes, making my two-hour workout well worth this pill I just swallowed. Determined and focused, I gave it my all, getting the best workout I had in years. I was exhausted, going hard sweating my ass off doing the last few sets of combinations on the heavy bag before I stopped.

I finished my workout and made my way to the locker room to get a quick shower and change clothes. I would head back to the office for a few hours to clear my head a little longer before I got home. I would definitely be addressing this situation with Emmanuel tonight. I just needed a little more time to calm down to say what I needed to say to him and not overreact and tear some shit up. I got out of the shower feeling fresh and liberated but deep down still pondering everything, trying to wrap my head around it all.

After I got dressed, I still needed to fix my hair and put on some lipstick before I left. I reached for my brush to brush my hair then it fell out of my makeup bag on the floor. While I bent down to pick it up, I heard voices from a group of young women entering the locker room, laughing extremely loud and animated as if someone told the joke of the year. They walked past me to a set of lockers behind mine to change, continuing their conversation about family and relationships, leaving me annoyed and now in even more of a rush to leave (college girls talked too much and too loud). I wasn't really paying attention to them at first, but when I listened in closer, one of the voices I heard speaking now sounded familiar to one I had heard so recent. I couldn't believe it! Could it be? I walked over to the mirror by the sink that faced their lockers to finish fixing my hair and to get a better view of this voice speaking. While I brushed my hair to put it in a ponytail, I looked back to make sure it was her behind me with her party of two. I only saw her from the side and the back in Emmanuel's office, but I recognized her hair, her look, and especially her voice. She had an accent. Italian, I think. Now with a full view of her, I paid close attention to her cheesing and smiling holding her conversation. She was about five foot ten, 150 pounds, long legs, and strong broad shoulders, hazel eyes, an olive complexion, and perfect teeth. I gotta admit, she was cute, had a nice figure, just not many curves. She was loud and excited; her conversation went on about how nervous she was for her family to meet her boyfriend. It was so much they did not approve from what she told them about him. In a worried and annoying tone of voice, she went on.

One of her friends said, "Why don't you tell your family who he is?"

"They won't approve of him being black. They won't approve of him being an older man, and I definitely know him being married won't help. I really don't know if we should be doing this, but I love him, and he loves me. I have faith in him that he will make our situation better for us to be together."

"Ha hmm, hmmm." I chuckled a little bit while I stood there in the mirror, hair finished, now packing up my makeup bag, listening to this desperate girl rant, knowing she was dead wrong trying to be with a married man she knew had a family. Content with how I looked now, ready to get out of there before I went crazy and interrupt and say something to this girl. I was doing my best not to say anything. I would deal with my husband when I got home since it was him who did me and our children wrong. I was not married to her. I walked past the girls to get to my locker, trying to smile and speak while I gathered the rest of my things by my locker. I silently heard snickering and whispering while I was putting my things up to go. On my way out, shaking my head, I heard Isabella mention something out loud with intentions for me to hear.

"*Well, she ain't enough for him no more anyway. It don't matter how much she works out!* He told me he needs more excitement, and believe me, baby, I give him that, and he loves it. I know his daughter is the only reason he's still there."

Then the bitch looked me right in my eyes and said, "His wife should just count her losses and move on because at this point, he's mine now."

I was standing there, listening to her talk shit about me, to me, in front of me, right now, talking about my family and throwing the fact that she was sleeping with my husband in my face in front of these college bitches like she about that life? *The fuck!* I was already mad, so I stopped and turned around, quick to respond.

"*What you say, bitch?* I know you ain't talking to me."

"I know who you are, Ms. Evelyn [*in a sarcastic tone*]. I know you're listening in on our conversation, and I saw you leave your husband's office today, listening earlier."

I had no recollection that she even knew who I was at first, and then I realized Emmanuel had a family picture on his desk in his office for her to know and see what I looked like.

"I didn't think I would meet you before Emmanuel was able to talk to you, but I think you should know from me that he and I are seeing each other, and we will be moving in together very soon and—"

At that moment, everything in me heated up, seeing only red and wanting blood. Before she could say another word, without even thinking in a rage, I just took off over to their locker, ready to fight. She tried to stand up on guard while she was in the middle of changing into a CSU team swimsuit when I threw my workout bag at her, watching her two girlfriends scatter out of the way when the bag hit her. It knocked her off-balance, giving me an open shot, connecting with a straight right punch to her cheekbone, then a two-hand mush to her face to the floor. She was stuck, speechless as she lay there holding her cheek, eye tearing up, fearing my next move. I was ready to continue my attack. She slid back on the floor, jogging pants still around her legs, surrendering and pleading. Realizing she was not in a position to defend herself or get help from her so-called friends, her next response was the dagger that changed everything.

"*You can't touch me. I'm pregnant!*"

Recovered and Ready (Diamond)

I'M ALMOST DONE healing and ready to get back on the search for India. It's been three days, and I'm feeling restless. I've talked to everyone I could back home and let them know I'll be back on campus as soon as possible. It's still summer, and my teammates got my back, so I ain't tripping on school at all. Mom contacted her older sister, my aunt Debbie, to let them know that I'm here under these situations and circumstances. I talked to her the other day when I got off the phone with Mom. She cussed my ass out too for not calling her, letting them know I'm here and all the shit that's going on. I haven't seen them in years, but we do talk often or as much as we can. I mean, we Facebook, Instagram, and all that. I do know they got my back all day though. This family, we gon' find my sister. They are on the way to pick me up now that I'm finally cleared to leave. I can't say that I'll miss this nothing-but-bad-memories-filled hospital.

Debbie was the oldest aunt of the sisters; she was brought up just like Mom in a two-parent family household. Both my grandparents went to college and worked. My grandfather, Sherman Meyers Jr., worked as an insurance agent, and my grandmother, Hope Edwards-Meyers, worked in banking. They instilled education, discipline, integrity, and even the right man to date. Everything Mom and her sisters needed to know for them to be successful with a healthy family. But for some reason, Aunt Debbie still managed to marry a dope boy from the hood. She was attracted to guys who grew up hard in the streets even though she wasn't from there. Square working dudes or even jocks were not her type of man. Debbie felt like it balanced her out having someone who lived an opposite lifestyle. Although, the catch-22 to that was her life and marriage between the last twenty years with this kind of man was always on and off. He was just in and out of prison so much. He's doing a ten-year bid now, but this time, it's because of his shady lawyer. Derek got set up by the feds to get back the money his lawyer owed the mob. A lot of money I hear it was.

Debbie Meyers's childhood boyfriend/man/kids' father/significant other/boss, Derek York, was a high yellow short, baldhead, built dude from Houston, Texas, who came to Ohio when crack got popular back in the '80s. Prison tattoos of gang signs all over his chest and back. The brotha was always dressed in black. He hardly ever smiled, slept, or did business anywhere by his home. In the streets, though, D was not the guy to fuck with. They said back in the day, a guy name Sam Smooth owed him like $50,000 in cash and dope and tried to skip town and not pay up. What D and his crew decided to do was send a message around town that they were not to be messed with. They went to this guy's mother's house where Sam's brother, his daughter, grandson, and mother lived. They broke into the house in the middle of the night, crept in everyone's room, and smashed everybody's head in with sledgehammers. All closed caskets. No one fucked with him ever since, and Aunt Debbie loved that gangsta shit about him. He always made sure he kept them financially safe and secure with everything. Their lifestyle was similar to ours as far as being spoiled; they just did it the hood ghetto fabulous way. She was ride or die too, new luxury car every year, hustling, having rental property around town, and working as a GM at the Doubletree Hotel downtown. He was known to do her transactions sometimes at work through booking rooms for her suppliers and clientele. All their three children have over six figures in their bank account. Derek Jr., who was the oldest at twenty-four, then their daughter, Dameka, who was a twenty-two-year-old geology major studying abroad in

Morocco, Africa. Dennis was the youngest. He was a twelve-year-old computer whiz.

Today, she was bringing the oldest, my cousin Derek Jr., with her to get me. He was the spitting image of his daddy, next in line to take over the family business He was solid, mean, with corn rolls and swag. He been boxing since he was six years old and never liked showing out, but he always had to knock niggas out because those who didn't know him used to think he was a soft pretty boy (wrong!). Like when I was nine and he was twelve years old playing football in front of our grandparents' house in Shaker Heights, Eddie from over on Buckeye got mad at DJ for talking to this girl he liked. Thinking it was a good idea to call DJ out to fight because he brought his cousins, Boy ended up embarrassing himself by getting put to sleep with a two-piece (wrong!).

Since basketball season is over and it's nothing else to watch on TV, I'm sitting in a chair in my room watching poker on ESPN, killing time until they get here. I'm fully dressed, feeling a whole lot better and ready to go. Hungry as shit, I told Aunt Debbie on the way to stop at McDonald's and bring me something to eat before we all go and speak with Detective Jones face-to-face to see how much information he has about my sister. From what DJ told me, he checked a few of his resources around town to see if any of his people knew anything but came up with nothing. Nobody in the family has seen or even heard from India yet since she left North Carolina and came here, which makes me really nervous. About an hour of waiting passed, and now I'm falling to sleep, bored and hungry. Then all of a sudden, DJ and Aunt Debbie walk in.

"Get yo ass up, cuz! What's going on, boy?"

"What's going on, man? I'm just chilling here, waiting on y'all to show up."

I get up off the bed to rush and give my cousin a handshake and hug to embrace each other out of love and respect.

"Cuz, now you know I love you, but what was you thinking trying to come here unknown and just be asking muhfuckas you don't know information about muhfuckas here? It's crazy in the land, man. You can't be doing that shit."

"I know I should have called somebody, got me in this muh-fucka. Your boy didn't have no burner or nothing. I was tripping. I don't know what I was thinking either. I was just so fucked up with all that happened that I was just asking everybody I saw about India. Let me see that though."

"I got you now. You ain't gotta worry about shit! For real!"

"I appreciate that too."

Derek Jr. hands me my bag of food and orange drink as I snatch it out of his hand impatiently, waiting to get to those fries. I then go over and hug Aunt Debbie and do the same thing, but her embrace was a lot longer and more nurturing. She knows what we all went through and hates seeing it all come to this.

"How you doing, baby? You feeling okay. You know your mother will be here on Tuesday?"

"I talked to her. Yeah, she told me you got us a suite at your hotel. Thank you, Auntie. I want some of them doubletree cookies too! Man, it's good to see y'all."

"It's good to see you too. You need me to get anything for you?"

I reach down and grab my stuff to go and then stop and realize something.

"Naw, I got it. Damn, I forgot, too, my bag with the rest of my stuff is in my rental car at Club Secrets on the Westside. I got here at night the other day, and that's the last place I parked. We can go there after we talk to the detective though. I'm ready to go now."

"All right, let's roll. I'm driving."

* * *

We make our way out of my room, heading to the elevator, when I pause for a moment, feeling a deeper level of nostalgia thinking about the look on Mom's face ten years ago when she ran down this very hallway from my father. DJ and Auntie look at me and ask if everything is okay as I get myself together, assuring them I'm good as we all enter the elevator to leave.

Behind the wheel of Auntie's 2014 candy-apple-red Benz truck, rolling through the streets of Cleveland with the music bumping on this sunny summer day, we all take a moment to vibe and enjoy the ride. En route to the police station to talk to Detective Jones, I call and let him know I'm on my way. The phone rings three times.

"Detective Jones speaking."

"Hey, Detective Jones, sir, this is Diamond Williams from Arizona. I'm out of the hospital now, feeling better, and I was on my way to talk to you about my sister. Do you have a minute?"

"Sure, come on in. I've been doing some searching. I think I got something for you."

"All right, I'm on my way I'll be there in about ten minutes."

"Sure thing."

We pull up to the front of the station as I make my way out of the car to head inside and see what information Detective Jones has for me. I walk up to the door, about to enter, thinking DJ and Auntie are about to follow me inside when I look back and see both of them still sitting in the vehicle.

"Y'all ain't coming in with me?"

"I mean, nephew, we do want to come in with you, but we spent so much time in and out this place dealing with Derek Sr. and his situation we just stop coming into anybody's police station. So for the time being, you go in there and talk to who you gotta talk to. We a be out here waiting for you, or if you need us to, we can go and get that rental car you left over there at Club Secrets. It ain't that far from here."

"I can come and get you, cuz. We legit over here."

"Yeah, that's cool. Go head. Here go the keys right here. It's a black Sonata. I called the owner the other day and told him that I would be there to pick it up today."

"All right, cousin, we a be back. I'm gon' make some more calls for you too about lil sis, see what the streets know. Call us when you ready, but we a be back ASAP."

"Okay."

I walk inside the station to get through metal detection and make my way to the elevator for the seventh floor where Detective Jones's office is. Right off the elevator around the corner, I head into the homicide department. The door is already open as I walk up to let him know I'm there. He is sitting at his desk in deep concentration, reading a file inside a folder. Looking down, adjusting the glasses on his face, and reaching for his cup of coffee that was placed next to him without noticing me, I get his attention.

"Knock knock! Hey, what's going on, Detective Jones?"

"Hey, what's up, Diamond? How's everything?"

"I'm all right, feeling better, still healing, but I'm a fighter. I just got in touch with some of my family here to help me find out what's going on. You said you had some information for me?"

"Yeah, I do. Have a seat."

Anxious to know what he has to say that could help me find out about India, I casually make my way to the two chairs sitting in front of his desk. Not 100 percent yet, so I slowly gather and adjust my position to sit still, feeling the pain in my healing ribs that were cracked just a few days ago.

"What's up?"

"I spoke with a few of my resources from the South who gave me some information about your father."

"Well, I do know he died from liver cancer from drinking so much. My mom told me he probably had it 'cause it was hereditary in his family. I haven't seen him and my sister in a few years, and now it's hurting me knowing I won't be able to see him again."

"When I read your chart the day they brought you in, I noticed your name and realized I knew who your people were. I went to school back in the day with your mother and father. Me and your dad played high school basketball together. He was our starting point guard. He even took us to state. They called him Emmanuel 'Handles' Williams. The boy was cold. I played the 3…yeah, that was my dog. Your mother, though, man. Every guy around town wanted to get with her and her sister's boy, them Meyers sister! Debbie still messing with Derek?"

I laugh it off and change the subject, wondering how much more about my family this guy knows, especially now that he's asking me questions about Aunt Debbie.

"I don't know nothing about that. I been in Arizona, and I came here to find out about my sister, sir. What about my father do you know?"

"From what I hear, he was teaching at a small community college there called Blue Ridge as an English teacher like he was here at Cleveland State. Through more investigating, we found out he was terminated from the college because he was caught messing around with a student."

"How could that be a problem? Wasn't she grown?"

"Well, it wasn't that she was just a student. He was supposedly caught messing around with the dean's daughter. She was some little young nineteen-year-old rich white girl majoring in communication. Her name was Tiffany Rothstein. She was Dean Eric Rothstein's daughter. He was a wealthy, arrogant, well-known businessman and undercover grand wizard of the many white supremacist groups there. Extremely connected throughout the state with enough pull to get your father fired and slander his name just like that. They tell me that Eric and your father never really got along, so when he found out about his daughter and Emmanuel fucking around, he forced little Tiffany to admit to and accuse your father of rape. Everybody around town knew this girl was a flaming hoe, and even though your father was later acquitted because of lack of evidence, it dragged on for so long that Emmanuel's reputation was never the same around town after. He was so devastated that he began drinking and gave up teaching."

"What about my sister though? What was she doing during all of this?"

"Her high school records show she was attending classes at a private school, and she was also taking some early college business courses at the same community college your father taught at. Your sister was an honor student at her prep school that was excelling in so many ways, one of the brightest in her class. With this rape charge going on, she just out of the blue dropped out and stopped attending school, period. The backlash received from reporters around the house, her classmates, and your father losing his job became so overwhelming India disappeared even from Emmanuel, and now no one knows what happened to her since."

I am feeling pretty good knowing that my dad, like mom and me, kept her studying her ass off to get through school. Upset though because his personal issues affected her to the point of being MIA.

"Damn, baby sis was doing her thing. So when did all this happen?"

"Almost two years ago and your father passed away a little over nine months. Like I told you, we haven't found any more information on your sister after that, and that could be a problem now."

"How could it be a prob—? What you mean?"

"Well, you said she is nineteen now. That means she can legally change her name, meaning I'm gonna have to pull some more strings and/or we're gonna have to find other ways of finding her."

"Well, that's what we gon' have to do then."

"Okay, that's about all I got for you right now, but I'll call you when I hear something else. You have my card, so you call me when you hear something 'cause I know your family. Y'all don't go doing more than y'all should to find your sister."

"For my sister, I'll do shit. We'll do whatever it takes, so I can't promise you nothing, Detective Jones."

"All right now, I'll be checking on y'all, making sure y'all staying out of trouble. I know how them York boys get down."

"That's cool. You have a good day, Detective Jones, and I'll be in touch."

"You too, Diamond Williams, starting point guard for UCLA. I know who you are."

"Cool. All right then."

I head out his office to the elevator feeling a little better with the information I just got. I know I have to be patient, but to hear she is doing well and that Dad kept her on it, I feel even more anxious to get to my sister. I know wherever she is right now, she's holding it down. I'll call Detective Jones when I get something.

I step outside to call my cousin and see where he at.

"Call DJ." Phone rings:

DJ picks up the phone and answers.

"Cousin! I was just about to call you. You talk to your boy?"

"Yeah, I talked to him."

"What that punk-ass nigga have to say?"

"Damn, I didn't know you ain't like dude like that. What's up with him?"

"You know my dad got locked up for some shit he didn't have nothing to do with because of that shady-ass lawyer Anthony Laria. So this corny-ass Detective Jones dude trying to be all gung ho on some save-the-streets bullshit was the one that got the word to lead his SWAT team to raid our house. Come to find out he had a thing for Mom all these years since high school, always trying to holler at her every time we would come to court or to the police station. Giving us his card, acting like he want to help when all he was really trying to do is get close to Mom. You can use this nigga if you want to find lil sis, but we got our own way of doing things here, cuz, for real."

"Good to know. If he can help me in any way, though, I'll use what he gives me, but other than that, I got what I need to know from him, so come on. I'm ready to do our own searching for India."

"All right, cuz, I'll be pulling up in a minute."

"Cool."

Chapter 7

Another Way

I SIT OUTSIDE the station for another ten minutes when DJ pulls up to get me in my rental, still intact and clean as I picked it up. I get in the car, and cuz is sitting there quietly and annoyed, listening to his lady on the phone complaining about something he can't get into full detail about right away. Not knowing or even caring for that matter that this is a nonsmoking rental, he pulls out a pack of Newport 100s, takes one out of the pack, lights it up, and takes a pull as if it were a way of exhaling the frustration in dealing with this woman on the other end of his line. He looks at me, shakes his head, gives me a slight smirk, and pulls off after I suggest he roll his window down to smoke.

"All right, I'll be there. Give me about an hour. I got to go and get my car, so I'll call you when I get home."

"All right, bye."

He hangs up the phone.

"Man, this girl crazy."

What's going on? Y'all good?"

"Well, I was supposed to pick up my daughter today, but since I heard you was in town, it slipped my mind."

"Awe, DJ, my bad, man. I didn't know. I appreciate you and Auntie coming to get me though. What's my beautiful little cousin's name? She yellow like you and yo daddy?"

"You know it's all good, cousin. We family. Her name is Faith. Daddy's little girl is three now, but no, nigga, she ain't yellow like me and my daddy. Her mother, Nora, is brownskin, so she brown like her. I had to let my fiancée know the reason you here and why I couldn't make it to pick up Faith. I know my baby girl is okay with her mother or her family. We got to find my little cousin."

"No doubt."

"She was cussing me out a little bit, but it's cool. Faith was just sad I didn't come. I'm about to go and get her after you drop me off. You wanna meet her?"

"Yeah, I wanna meet her. I ain't got nothing to do but see all the family."

"You can drop me off to my car and then follow me over my girls. Nora got this friend, Brittany, single who can come through. Somebody I think a be good for you to kick it with while you here."

"What she look like?"

"I ain't even gon' tell you. When you see her, just thank me."

"All right, I'ma take your word for it."

DJ smiles at me, finishes his cigarette, throws it out the window, turns the volume up to a Drake song bumping on satellite radio, and continues mobbing through downtown. We make our way east toward Shaker Heights so we can drop him off to his car at his apartment. In a rush, he tells me he will be right out, so I just get out the car for a minute, stretch my legs before I get in the driver's seat to sit, and wait for him to change. He comes out the house fifteen minutes later clean, now happy, as he walks to his white Beamer dressed in all white from cargo shorts to his Nike Air Maxes, a white tank top, wave cap, and an all-white Indians hat.

Opening up his door, cheesing, I recognize the swag but hate it on him anyway.

"Nigga, you ain't fresh. That's why yo shit gon' get dirty."

"Why you gotta hate, cuz? You know I'm clean. Ask ya momma, nigga."

"Awwww, why you gotta talk about mommas?"

"I'm fucking with you. Just follow me. She don't live that far."

"Lead the way. I'm behind you."

He gets in his car, turns up his system with the new Scarface playing, and speeds off down the street as I follow him a few blocks away from his spot to Nora's house over on Van Aken.

It's a hot and humid June evening, and I'm still feeling a little tired, doing my best to ignore the pain I still feel in my ribs and try to keep up with cuz, who is mobbing and bumping through this heavy traffic. We finally pull up to the house as I trail him into the driveway to see two ladies and DJ's daughter, Faith, sitting on the porch outside, talking. As I walk behind DJ onto the porch, he politely introduces me to his fiancée and soon-to-be wife, La Nora; his daughter; and her friend Brittany.

Brittany says, "How you doing? I'm Brittany. Nice to meet you."

"Hey, what's going on, Diamond? Nice to meet you too."

Very impressed by what I see and understanding what cousin was talking about now, I shake her hand softly and gaze directly into her eyes to assure her that I am interested. Natural features with no makeup, beautiful skin standing 5 foot 2, dark chocolate, wrapped in a blue-and-yellow sundress that shows every part of her voluptuous figure. Before pursuing her right away, I turn my attention to my cute little cousin and her momma to introduce myself to them.

"And who is this little cutie pie right here? Hi, I'm your cousin Diamond. What's your name?"

"My name is Faith. I'm outside hanging with my mommy, and I had ice cream today."

"Awww, did you? I like ice cream too."

"Hey, what's going on?"

La Nora replies, "Hey, how you doing? I'm La Nora. Sorry to hear about everything. You know we here for you."

"I appreciate that. Now that I'm with fam, I know we gon' find her."

DJ says, "Most definitely! Prayer ain't needed 'cause it don't matter what we gotta do. We gon' find my little cousin, A Diamond. Nora, cook some fried chicken, pasta salad, and some fruit. You want something to eat? I know you hungry."

"Of course I want something to eat. Hook it up!"

"All right, cool. We a be back. Come on, Fae Fae. We gon' go in the house. Daddy hungry. I want something to eat."

"Okay, Daddy. Bye, cousin Dime."

"Byeeee, don't forget to save me some ice cream, okay?"

"Okay."

"We gon' go and get you a plate, man. You two talk, exchange numbers, and get to know each other."

"All right, D, we got you."

Brittany says, "Bye, Derek."

DJ opens the screen door for his two ladies, letting them enter first to go and get us both something to eat and drink. I carefully adjust my position on the love seat, trying to get it together and find a way to spark up a conversation with Ms. Brittany.

"So are you originally from Cleveland?"

"Well, I'm actually from Stow, Ohio, but I was born in Nigeria. My mother and father moved my brothers and sisters and I to America when I was two years old for a better life. My last name is Bello, which means 'assistant.'"

"That's cool. Yeah, my mom named me Diamond because my father proposed to her when she was pregnant with me. She loved the ring so much she named me after that. Plus, I shine like one. Ha! How old are you?"

"You got jokes. That's cute. I'm twenty-three, a Pisces in every way, no children yet. I work as a cosmetologist at my girl's shop on Larchmere not too far from here. I'm also working on my master's as a business consultant at Cleveland State, so I'm here until something else better comes along after graduating."

"Wow, I can dig it, you—"

Before getting another word out, she interrupts me with her own questions and concerns.

"I'm sorry. We can talk about me later. I've heard a lot about you, Diamond, and what you've been through, and the fact that you're doing all this to find your little sister is so brave and sweet. Honestly, I just want to give you a hug. Can I give you a hug right now?"

Offset by her disruption but very much blown away by her willingness to comfort me in such an unusual situation, instantly, I feel her connection. If this is what they mean by love at first sight, then damn, she has caught my eye.

"Of course you can."

Brittany casually gets up out of her chair and walks up to me very close. She grins as she intentionally puts her DDs directly in my face while looking and smelling like heaven with open arms. Still sitting on the love seat, I then rise, towering over her short stature, to pull her close and embrace each other as if I've known her for years. How liberating this woman's touch is; I melt into her arms to hold tighter, enjoying the sweet smell of her perfume and the softness of her skin. We hold on and share a moment as long as we can before separating from each other's grasp, quickly as DJ and family walk out with my plate of food.

I finish my plate, play with Faith a little bit, and chop it up with them till about 11:00 p.m. or so. It is getting late, so I say my good-byes to everybody so I can head to the hotel and check into my room and rest a little bit. Brittany also decides that it is about time that she heads home herself. With an opportunity to exchange information, I feel obliged.

"I can walk you to your car, Momma, if you don't mind."

"Of course you can. I was gon' ask you anyway."

"Cool, all right, cousin, Nora. Tell the little one I'll see her soon. Thanks for the food too. Appreciate it."

"All right, cuz."

"Bye, y'all have a good night. I'm at you first thing in the a.m."

Brittany says, "Bye, y'all. Nora, I'ma call you tomorrow after I get off work. Bye, Derek."

DJ says, "All right, cool. Yeah, we gotta do some looking around tomorrow for real."

Nora follows behind us, waves her goodbyes, then locks the door after we walk out to leave.

Chapter 8

Me and Her

As WE STEP off the porch together, Brittany wraps her arm around mine, allowing me to get closer, still smelling as good as she did earlier while we walk side by side like a happy new couple to her car. We exchange numbers, then say our goodbyes with a hug and a kiss on the cheek. I watch her pull off, then I walk to my rental car shortly after to leave.

I'm twenty minutes into my drive, now pulling up to the hotel, when my phone starts ringing. Assuming its Mom or somebody from back home, I take my time to answer. But when I look to see who it is, to my surprise, it's Ms. Brittany calling me already. Excited that it's her, I hurry and answer before it goes to voice mail.

"What's going on, lady?"

"Hey, Diamond, I'm just calling you to let you know that I made it home. Now I'm trying to think of how to say this without sounding desperate, but I have been thinking about you since we left your cousins, realizing I am feeling you more than I thought I would. So what I was hoping was, well…do you feel it'd be too soon if I wanted to spend the night with you in your room…tonight?"

Excited and turned on that she is feeling me like I'm feeling her, I then pause for a moment to catch my breath before responding, too fast and eager myself.

"Hell, naw, it ain't. I mean, not at all. I don't think it would be too soon. I would actually love the company, especially you because honestly, I'm feeling you as well. I just pulled up to the hotel. I'm about to go check in, then get clean. I'll be here though."

"That's fine. I'm just getting out the shower myself. I'll be finished soon, and I could be there in about forty-five minutes, if that's okay with you?"

"It's all good with me, baby. Give me a call when you close, and I'll meet you downstairs."

"I definitely will. Bye, Diamond."

"Bye, Brittany. See you in a minute."

I hang up the phone, then check the time.

"Okay, it's a quarter to midnight, and I got a booty call on my first night in the room. Let's get it."

Excited and now in a rush, I pull in the parking deck to the hotel to check in my two-room executive suite. I grab my bag from out the trunk and then check my pockets to make sure I have everything. To my surprise, I realize that I already have the key to my room, forgetting Aunt Debbie gave it to me when they picked me up earlier.

"Sweet. I can just go straight to my room now. Time saved."

I urgently make my way into the building, enter the elevator, and head to the ninth floor and exit the elevator and to my room. I walk in the door, toss my bags on the couch, and jump in the shower right away. I got to wash all of the anxiety, pain, and sweat that I accumulated from being in this humid Ohio heat all day. I get out the shower, put on my basketball shorts, no boxers, a tank top, and a spray or two of my favorite cologne, Sean John. I then relax a little bit comfortably on my king-size bed, watch some TV, and kill some time before Ms. Brittany calls me.

About 12:15 a.m., my phone rings. I pick up.

"Hey, hey, what room are you in?"

This woman is downstairs, already in the lobby, asking me for details on how to get to the room.

"That was fast. You are prompt, I see. I like that. I'll be down in a minute to meet you, Momma."

"Okay."

I head downstairs to escort her back to my room so we can relax, converse, and/or whatever is on her mind to do to end this night. I arrive in the lobby area to see her sitting on one of the couches, waiting for me. She stands up to greet me with another hug, this time dressed in a black sundress, fitting as if she painted it on really, cleavage showing, and ass extruding out of her dress. The front desk agent and every man walking past us can't do nothing but stare as we make our way to the elevator. I have to admit, she is looking even more irresistible tonight than she did earlier.

We get to my room door, impatiently waiting to be alone. I open it and allow her to walk in, following right behind her to close and lock the door. As soon as I turn around from doing so, she slowly walks over to me and gives me a hug and a long passionate kiss.

"I brought us some wine. You wanna have drink with me real quick?"

"Sure, what you got?"

"I was gon' bring some liquor, but I ran out. All I got is some pink moscato. It's good though."

"I'm good with that. Let me see that. I'ma just take it to the head."

We pass the bottle back and forth, taking shot like swings, intensifying the moment for what our bodies both want from each other. *Passion!*

After our fourth shot, I take the bottle and sit it down on the table. As soon as I turn around from doing so, she slowly walks over to me and gives me another hug and a long passionate kiss. Heart and blood racing to every area in my body, my hands quickly wrap around her twenty-seven-inch waist, then slowly sliding down to her round, soft, but firm forty-two inches of ass that, from gripping, is without panties on. We continue to kiss as I guide us to my bed in the other room. She helps me take off my tank top, and I gently lay her on the bed. I then lift her dress up as she lies on her back on the edge of the bed, allowing me to spread her legs open, giving me a full view of her already wet and shaved flower.

Instantly stimulated, I make my way to taste and enjoy her sweet juices all over my tongue. I continue licking and kissing around her walls, putting my tongue inside, then sucking on her clit while she moans and squirms in complete satisfaction. I was born with that GOG (gift of gab), so I aim to please. I move up to her stomach and to her chocolate-brown breasts. I start sucking on one nipple while caressing the other, then I switch up. I lick and kiss up to her neck to kiss her lips again. Kissing my way back down town to pleasure her for another ten minutes, adding my fingers until she reaches one of her soon-to-be many orgasms, screaming, turning me on even more.

"I'm coming! I'm coming! *Yes! Yes!*"

I laugh a little bit while she's laying there shaking for a moment, then she gets back up to show me some mutual love. She helps me take off my shorts, then gets up to straddle me, placing her body all over mine, kissing me from my lips down to my chest to my stomach. Pleased by what she sees, she grabs my nine and a half, kisses the head, then puts it halfway down her throat and does the best she can to go all the way while using her hands to stroke it. Five and a half minutes of her sucking, stroking, gagging, and doing her thing and with me about to bust a big one, I stop her so we can start intercourse. I grab my phone to put on some music. She gets in missionary position and plays with her pussy, awaiting my next move. I put the phone down as R. Kelly's "It Seems Like You're Ready" begins to play on my Spotify's Passion playlist. I stop to stare for a moment at this beautiful naked, voluptuous, chocolate Nubian goddess ready and waiting for me while I stand by the bed, fully erect.

I get on top of her, staring directly in her eyes before slowly entering her warm, soft, and wet walls. She gasps. "*Ahh!*" I smirk and pull out a little, then go in deeper, forcing her eyes close and her walls to cream even more as she pulls me closer, body to body. We explore every position from missionary to doggy style to her riding me, front and back, and even on both of her sides. Our connection and attraction gives us the energy to fuck on and off most of the night, just to wake up in the morning and do it again. Damn, this feels good to be back home.

More than Enough

SUNDAY, 10:06 A.M., mind racing and body rejuvenated about what just took place last night and still earlier this morning, I roll over to check my phone for all the missed texts and phone calls coming in while Brittany and I were doing our rounds. She feels me move, so she scoots over closer and puts her arm around me.

"Good morning."

"Hey, good morning. How you feeling?"

"I'm great, thank you. I really needed that."

"Yeah, me too. That's the best thing to happen to me since shit a while. Damn, Momma done gave me some energy and shit. Thank you!"

I give her a wink, pull the sheets off me, get up out of the bed, and walk into the bathroom to use it, wash my face, and brush my teeth. Brittany gets up shortly after and follows me in, quickly grabbing her washcloth and washing her face in front of the mirror. I, on the other hand, do my best in front of the toilet to aim and get my manhood at the right angle to get it all in the bowl while still suffering from morning wood.

"You want to go and get some breakfast? I'm buying."

"After you done put me to work all night, of course I would love some breakfast. Auntie hooked everything up though, so we can eat downstairs. We don't have to pay. We good, Momma."

"Good, 'cause I'm starving, but before I go home, can we come back up to the room and do it one more time, just one more time?"

"Do you really gotta ask? For real? It's all about you right now, B."

"That's good to know. I feel the same way."

"Yes, ma'am."

We handle our business in the bathroom, put some clothes on, head downstairs, pick up some breakfast, and bring it back upstairs and eat it in my room. We finish our food and then go at it like animals as we planned one more time. While getting dressed again, I begin telling Brittany the details of my situation, like what was going on and why I'm back here in Cleveland. I even tell her about what happened to me the other night at the strip club. As I am giving her a vague description of the club and about the guys who attacked me, she mentions that she knows one of them from a previous relationship. She also says that she knows that he still works at the same club. Now I'm intrigued. I could definitely use some more information, so I quickly put a rush on us leaving. We finish getting dress, then make our way out the room around 1:30 p.m. We head downstairs, pass the lobby area and out to our cars, conversing about last night and a few other things and us when I casually change the subject.

"So back to this guy. What's old dude's name from the club? What's up with him?"

"His name is Cordell Ross. It's two of them that's tall though. He the one that's like six foot six, 260–270 pounds stocky, dark skin with a bald head."

"Yeah, that's one of 'em. That nigga pushed me out the door first."

"He used to be a high school football all-state defensive end, but he kept playing around in college with the girls, not studying think-ing, football was gon' be his life. He end up getting hurt, then kicked out of school for failing his classes. Now he's a bouncer slash hustler, I guess. He still likes me, but that chapter of my life is closed. Usually though, when I've been around him, he's acting silly or clowning around. I don't know why he would have did that to you if you wasn't being all drunk and crazy 'cause that's not him. Somebody must have told him to do it. Then again, he is Haitian, and they can be crazy at times, so I don't really know."

"He Haitian? For real, do he got any other family here?"

"Yeah, he got like two other brothers who just as big as him. One of 'em is in jail right now, though, for murder. Richard, he the oldest, and the other one, Cedric, he work there as a bouncer too. He the other tall one with dreads."

"Yeah, that nigga too, punk ass."

"And it's two sisters. I think one of 'em just moved back here from Columbus or somewhere in the South. Her name is… Dah, Dah, D something."

"Is it Delilah?"

"Yeah, I think it is Delilah. Yeah, and the other sister's name is Eleanor, something basic. How you know about Delilah?"

"India, my sister, used to be with a female named Delilah all the time when I would talk to her on the phone a while back. Both being from Ohio, they could relate to each other, so from what India told me, they got close real quick. I wonder if she's the same Delilah."

"You think she is?"

"I don't know, but what I do know is, we gon' do whatever we got to do to find my sister. If this family know anything about anything, if anybody in this club know anything about anything, we gon' find out. I personally asked those cats about India that night. I wasn't trying to start no trouble, but they attacked me anyway. So if I gotta go see this nigga, who or whatever other football playing-ass niggas he know, I'ma go see them and they family with me and my family this time. We gon' bring a whole lot of artillery with us too. They could have ruined my basketball season, career, or killed me, man! I was just trying to find my sister. I don't know what that shit was about."

"Well, I have his number in my phone, Diamond. What or how do you want to handle this?"

"Call him and get some more information. See what's up with his sister and who she roll with and all that, then call me. Let me know whatever night he gon' be at the club next too 'cause we going. I was trying to come here to find my sister, but we can't let this shit go, so with that, I'm about to get out of here and go see cuz, but don't forget to call me and let me know what's up"

"I got you, Diamond. I'll do whatever I can to help."

"That's good to know. So when can I see you again?"

"Whenever you want to, baby."

"It'll be sooner than later, Momma."

"I hope so."

"Yes, ma'am."

We smile, say our goodbyes, and send each other off with another big hug and a kiss on the lips. She gets in her car, and I do the same as we both head in our own direction. I feel better now that I'm getting somewhere with my sister's whereabouts. Brittany was just a bonus. Appreciate cuz too for hooking me up with her. While I'm thinking about it, let me call this dude.

Chapter 10

Getting Reacquainted

Phone rings.

DJ answers, "*Hello.*"

"What up, D!"

"Diamond, what up, cuz. I tried to call you this morning. What yo ass been doing?"

"I was getting some very much-so-needed rest, man. Baby girl came to chill with me last night too."

"Baby girl who? Brittany? I know you ain't talking about Ms. Good Girl Brittany? Whaaat!"

"Yeah, man, she a sweetheart. After your girl told her about my situation and of course my irresistible charm, baby been throwing it at me since I step on the porch yesterday. Hugging me all long and affectionate when y'all went in the house and shit."

Uh Uhh, Dime, for real? For real though, cousin, you got a good one. She ain't easy, man, at all. With all that body, all kinds of men be trying to get at her everywhere she go, but she be turning 'em down. She like to mess with dudes from out of town now."

"Man I got to give you props for this woman 'cause *damn*! I mean, she do her thing, man. She do her muthafucking thing! I couldn't, well, we couldn't keep our hands off each other. We was at it all night. The chemistry is crazy. She just left the hotel when I left."

"I see she was feeling you, but damn, I didn't know like that. I'm tripping. She was just on it, huh?"

"That ain't even the good part though. She know one of the cats that jump me at the bar that night. Dude and his brother work there, two big-ass bouncer dudes. Peep this. They got a sister named Delilah that just came from the South. India had a girl she hung out with named Delilah that she used to kick it with down South that's from Ohio. She Haitian just like these two niggas."

"Yeah.",.

"Yes, sir."

"What you wanna do?"

"I wanna go to the club and talk to these niggas again. Find out where the fuck my sister at, by any means muthafuckin' necessary."

"Let's do it. Meet me at my house."

"I'm on my way."

I'm on it now, putting a little more pedal to the metal so I can get to Shaker Heights and come up with this plan to go and see these brothers who put one on me the other night. I get to D's house, its cars all in his driveway and all in front of his spot like he was having a party or something. Knock on the door to be greeted by one of D's homeboys, nicknamed Dolo, coming from his enormous size of 6'9", 350 pounds, meaning he can fuck some shit up by his self (solo).

Dolo says in a deep voice, "What's up, man."

"Hey, what's going on, big man?"

I give him a pound and walk past into the living room where about eight other brothas and some females was sitting around. They was bumping music, playing NBA 2K14, talking shit while smoking and drinking. Derek is in his dining room sitting at the table, smoking on his own blunt and cleaning off some guns, talking to some other people hanging out in the kitchen. He sees me come in and calls me over.

"Ah, cuz, what's up? Come check this shit out."

"Y'all mufuckas kicking it, I see. What you got there?"

D pulls out a Kel-Tec KSG 14 round 12 gauge to show me how ready he and his team is down to help find lil sis.

"This that tear the club up shit right here, Diamond. We ain't playing! Everybody in this city know how I get down. I'm into everything, man, from dope to weed to guns to credit cards. You name it, and I'm hustling it. Pops instilled this shit in me. I know it ain't politically correct or whatever the fuck that means, but we survive how they survive."

"I see. Why you don't give me that Glock 19 right there though. I like that one."

"Look, we not going in strapped. We going in deep though some men, some women, like we there to have a good time. It's gon' be some more of y'all outside waiting and chilling a little longer to come in. We gon' go in there with the intent to understand their reason for fucking with you for asking about your sister that day. If I don't like how they respond or their reason, it is what it is after that. You can chill outside with them 'cause I don't want you to get into too much of our world. You gotta that reputation from playing ball and shit, so I'ma need you to lay low. Our moms a kick my ass if I get you in trouble again like back in the day."

"That's cool. I'll chill, but you got to make sure we find out where India is or as much as you can without fucking shit up too much. My pop's neighbor told me when I was in North Carolina her friend Delilah was a dance major. He said she would come back home to Ohio and do some stripping on the side to pay for school. When they jumped me, it let me know I was in the right place. I checked over five different clubs here first. That's the main reason I came back here to this club. I'ma need for y'all to check for her first, then check them niggas."

"I got you, Dime. Hold on. *Aye!* Listen up!"

Derek stands up and walks over to the doorway of the living room dining room. Everybody in the living room and the few in the kitchen rolling up and conversing stop what they're doing to listen to D.

"Y'all hear that. We gon' be chill till I give y'all the word. Don't nobody do shit. We looking for a chick named Delilah. She dance there. She know something about where my little cousin India is. Her brothers are bouncers there though, so look for her first. If we don't find her, we talking to them, and that's when we can fuck some shit up. Y'all got me"?

"We got you D."

"Yeah."

"Hell yeah."

"Okay."

"No doubt."

"You want something to drink, Dime? Smoke? We got it all, cuz, pills, whatever you need."

"I usually don't when I'm training, but since I'm here, let me hit that L. Just once, though. Clear my head for a minute. I'm good on the drink and everything else though."

"It's all good, cousin. We got you, like I said. Only thing now is we got to go shopping."

"Shopping for what?"

"Clothes, nigga. It's Sunday, so we about to leave in a minute. Tonight we all wearing black."

"I can dig that. Where we going?"

"I'ma try Urban Wear over there on Buckeye, but if they closed, we going somewhere else. Shit, I don't care. I got boosters if everybody closed by the time we get there. It's all on me too, Dime. Blacked out is how I like to roll when I'm deep. We gon' be fly and shit. No T-shirts and corny hood clothes. Some expensive attire. You 'bout ready to go?"

"Yup."

"All right, let's do it."

Before leaving, we make sure everyone was on the same page about what is going to take place tonight when we get to Club Secrets. Crew finishes cleaning, loading, and stocking everything needed for tonight, then follows behind us out the door. The plan is for everybody to go get dressed, meet back up at D's, recharge the buzz, and then go out to the club twenty deep.

Me and D go to a few places around town to pick out me and him some black attire for tonight. We grab some pants from here, shirts from there, get something to eat, and complete our search a little after eight o'clock. Rolling, feeling good in his white Beamer back to his house to change and get ready, my phone starts to ring. It's Momma.

"Hey, Ma, what's up?"

"What y'all down there getting into? You hear anything about your sister yet?"

"Yeah, I'm checking on some things tonight. Gotta meet up with some people. I did talk to this detective dude, though. Detective Jones, he said he played ball with Dad. DJ told me he used to and still always trying to get with Aunt Debbie. You know him?"

"Yeah, I know him, Steven Jones. He's been chasing your aunt for years. I didn't know he became a detective though, hmm. Well, I was just calling you to let you know that I will be there on Tuesday to see everybody. You talk to your grandmother yet?"

"Naw, I ain't have a chance to, but we can go and see her together when you get here. I'm with D now about to go out tonight to check on some thangs about sis."

Derek, in the background, says, "Hi, Aunty."

"Tell that crazy boy I said hey, but I hear you, Diamond. You keep me posted about what's going on. Me and Troy out getting something to eat right now, probably go do some more shopping tomorrow for my trip back home. I'll see you guys in a few more days, baby."

"All right, Ma. Talk to you later."

"Bye, bye."

DJ says, "I just texted crew. I told them to meet back up at ten o'clock. We about to pick up some more blunts, then head back."

"That's cool, man. I'm feeling good. Just got some fresh gear, and I'm about to go see some ass later on. Let's get it!"

"Hell yeah."

Chapter 11

Club Secrets

AFTER LEAVING DOWNTOWN Tower City, playing some slots and grabbing a few more things, we head back 480 East to Shaker Heights to get dressed and ready. After we get back to his house, I get in the shower first to get myself together. While finishing ironing my clothes, getting ready in the second bedroom, I get a text from Brittany.

"Sorry getting back so late. Got caught up with family. I talked to Cordell though, and he said he will be at work tonight. We didn't talk long, but he does have a sister named Delilah who did just move back here from North Carolina, and she works at the club. This sounds like her, Diamond. What now?"

I text back, "We about to head out that way in a few. We deep, men and women, trying not to start no drama but definitely ready for it. Just going to ask some questions if we see her. If we don't, we asking them."

"Okay, be safe. Hope to hear from you soon."

"I'll call you tonight, if that's cool?"

"Yes, it is."

"Cool. It'll be sooner than later."

"I'll be waiting on you, Daddy."

I hang up the phone and rushed to get dressed. Crew starts coming back through a little after 9:30, with everybody dressed in their own grown and sexy black attire and party favors in hand (blunts and liquor). I come out of the bedroom feeling fresh, dressed in an all-black Rocawear linen suit, black tank top, black ankh medallion, with the all-black LeBrons and an all-black Indians baseball cap. I'm in a great mood, ready to enjoy myself around loved ones. I walk out to the living room where everyone is to get myself at least one shot. Everybody, including DJ, is standing in a circle, blacked out, ready to say a prayer and make a toast. They pour me a shot of Patrón as I walk up.

DJ says, "Hey, Diamond, come in here. We all here for you, man. Everybody in here know what it's like to lose a loved one in some kind of way. Tonight we go out and do what we can to get some leads on finding lil cuz, by any means muthafucking necessary."

DJ hands me the shot as we all raise our glasses, gathered around each other in a circle.

"All right, I just want to say thank ya'll for being here for me, going out ya'll way to help me. May the Most High be with us and guide us in the right direction to finding India peacefully, but if not, may all of us be safe in our endeavors to do so. To family!"

Everybody says, "Family!"

We take a few more shots, hit a few more blunts, then round up all that's needed before we go. Everybody is buzzed and turned up. We pack in about nine cars and head west to Club Secrets to have a good time. I get in the car and roll with DJ, of course, who's dressed in an all-black hooded Gucci sports track jogging suit. Feeling ourselves kicking it, hanging out the car and still smoking on the highway, mobbing with crew, clowning, switching lanes behind us. We finally get to the club around 11:20 even more turned up, ready to see some dancers and get some more drinks.

DJ says, "All right, Diamond, we about to go check out the scene in here and see what we can find out. Me, Dolo, Rob, Black, Meech, Reese, Big Sam, and a few of the ladies gon' go in first. Give it about fifteen minutes, then come right in behind us. I'ma pay for everybody, so y'all can just walk right in. Have them walk around you so nobody will see you. We a be too deep for them to notice you right away."

"I got you."

We get out and wait for everybody to walk up and huddle around us by DJ's car to go over the plan. D and them start walking in while the rest of us sit outside by his car to finish off the rest of these blunts and talk for a minute. While sitting outside, chopping it up with the ladies with us and waiting to go in, I have an idea. Tori is one of the three females I am talking to. She is about five foot one, light-brown skin, a fat ass on her slim but thick figure to go with a cute face. She is on it too, and I will holler at her if Brittany isn't so damn perfect for me. I pull her to the side for a minute.

"Hey, what's up, Tori? Let me holla at you?"

"What's up, Diamond?"

"When we go in here, I'm a need you to chill at the bar for a minute and ask about Delilah. Try to get a dance when you catch her or buy her a drink. See if you can find out information like where she live and who she hang with. Women tend to open up more to women than men. Can you do that for me, Momma?"

"No problem, baby, I got you. You know what she look like?"

"I don't. That's why I don't want to ask around no more 'cause her brothers know what I look like. We want to try and find her first though."

"That's cool. Me and Kiana gon' go. She like girls anyway, so I'll let her know what's going on."

Kiana "Kia" Sweets dresses, talks, and tries to walk like a dude, but she is so damn cute you know she is a girl. Light skin with blond locks, green eyes and a petite figure. Social, charming, with a sweet personality. D has her around for other reasons though. Although she is cool calm and collected, she is his best-kept secret in the game. Kiana is known as Crew's silent assassin. She does hits for him whenever he needs some business handled he doesn't want to be linked to.

"Okay, I'm cool with that. I'ma be somewhere in the cut. Just give me the word when you spot her."

"Will do."

About ten minutes of conversing and waiting, DJ sends a group text for us all to come in. We get the word and start heading inside. Karan, Amp, Mike, Tori, Kiana, and Big Tina crowd around me as we calmly walk through the door past the sexy brown-skin female at the entrance collecting money to enter. She recognizes that we're the group who's fee is already paid for by DJ earlier and just smiles as we all walk past.

I, Mike, Karan, and Big Tina walk to the smoking area so I can lay low and act like I'm smoking a mild with them as everybody else go inside to the bar and stage area to get drinks and watch the ladies perform. By this time, DJ, Dolo, and Amp are throwing money at the women on stage. Karan and Meech head upstairs to get private dances. The ladies are all at the bar ordering champagne and drinks for us, observing the scene. I look around to see if any of these ladies is Delilah. I used to know what she looks like, but it's been so long since I've seen her I can't remember. Still not sure who is who, I still take the time to enjoy the atmosphere anyway. So many flavors of women looking just as thick and juicy as they wanna be, enticing every man and woman around them, getting that money while doing it.

I'm sitting down talking to Mike about sports when one of the dancers comes out and sits down next to me to take a break and smoke for a minute. She politely asks if she can sit down and introduce herself.

Hi, can I sit here?"

"Of course."

"I'm Honey, by the way. How you doing?"

I reach out to shake her hand, then assist with my lighter to help her with her cigarette.

"How you doing, Honey? I'm D."

"Nice to meet you."

"Nice to meet you too. You looking good, Ms. Honey. I see you."

"Thank you, thank you. You get any dances from any of the girls here yet?"

"I will soon, marinating for a minute. How's your night been?"

"It's been cool so far. Now that more people are coming in, it should get better."

"It will. I may want a dance from you myself when we both go inside."

"Okay, just let me know."

We chop it up a little while longer when she stops for a minute and looks at me real hard. I look back at her real hard, then notice Tori walking in.

"You look familiar. I seen you somewhere before. You from around here?"

"Naw, this my first time here. I…what's happening, lady?"

While in the middle of talking to her, Tori walks up, stands next to Honey, says hello to her, then hands me a Grey Goose and pineapple (my drink when I go out) and sits down beside me. Not knowing who she is, Honey gets up and allows Tori to sit down.

"I'm a head back in now. Nice talking to you, D. I'll see you inside."

"All right, lady. I'll be in there."

Honey takes her last puff of her smoke and walks back inside to freshen up before she makes her rounds again. Karan and Big Tina get up and walk out behind her to go in and get some drinks.

Karan says, "Hey, D, we going in."

"All right y'all, I'll be in in a minute."

Tori says, "What's up, Diamond? What she say?"

"Who, old girl?"

"She just introduced herself. I told her I was gon' get a dance from her later. Her name was Honey."

Tori gets closer to whisper in my ear.

"I was asking the bartender about all the girls in here, trying to check for you like you asked. I came out here because she was just telling me that Honey, the girl that just walked inside, is Delilah!"

Shocked and tripping now because I feel a little nostalgia looking at her but can't really tell, being as tipsy as I am. I pause for a second, then respond without trying to make a scene.

"For real! Baby girl that just walked out?"

"Yup."

"Damn! That's why she said I looked familiar."

"Yeah, that's her."

"Okay, I'm about to get a dance from her and see what I can find out. Go get DJ and let him know what's up."

"I'm on it right now."

We both get up and walk inside by the bar as I take a seat in the corner by the door to go upstairs in the private rooms. I put my hat down a lil more so my face ain't as recognizable to everybody. DJ and crew are on the other side of the room having a ball throwing more money, drinking and getting lap dances. Tori walks over to let him know what's up. He turns around to me and nods his head, looks at Sam, and continues doing what he's doing. Big Sam then walks over with Tori to sit a few tables over from me to keep his eye out. Chilling, now sipping on another drink, I see Honey/Delilah walk out (she is a little sexy-ass young lady). We make eye contact. I smile and wink to get her attention; she smiles back and begins walking in my direction. She takes a seat by me, pulls her seat closer, and crosses her legs in front of me.

I say, "You want a drink?"

Honey says, "Sure, amaretto sour."

"Got you."

I reach in my pocket and pull out a fifty dollar and give it to her to get a drink and tell her to keep the rest for the dance she gon' give me.

"You want another drink?"

"I'm cool with this. I'll be sitting over here waiting for you."

"Okay, I'll be right back. You sure I don't know you?"

I play it off and deny it.

"I don't think so. I ain't from around here."

I smile when she gets up and walks to the bar to get her drink. Looking flawless, made up, hair done, five-inch heels matching the blue laced panty and bra set she was wearing. Lil sister's friend is sexy, and I get to see what her little sexy ass is working with. I sit back and adjust myself to get ready for my dance. I'm chilling now, ready for her when I see Cedric come downstairs, walking past me to the bar area where Delilah is standing. He says a few things to her, then from what I can tell, she tells him she's about to give me a dance because as soon as she says something, they both look directly at me. Trying to get comfortable, I'm in the middle of taking my hat off and stretching when he looks and recognizes me right away. He tells Delilah to stay back and approaches my table.

Cedric says, "Don't I know you?"

My mood changes immediately to anger, not only for the other day but now for getting in the way of my dance with his sister. I ignore him, keep my head down, and reach for my drink while quickly getting myself ready to attack him if he gets any closer. He gradually gets closers and asks me the same question even louder for people to hear, trying to make a scene.

"A nigga, I know you heard me. Don't I know you from the other day?"

I look up and see Big Sam stand up. DJ and crew then turn around and observe the situation. His brother Cordell and another bouncer comes downstairs to back up Cedric. The rest of the crew come out and make their way around to my table, surrounding their staff. I then stand up, pissed now and ready to swing on this same dude who stomped me the other night. His size don't even matter at this point.

"Yeah, nigga, you know me. You bitch-ass niggas jumped me the other day while I was here just asking about my sister."

Cedric and Cordell look at each other, lost. I then look to the bar to see Honey's (Delilah's) face turn to stone as well. She looks at me and says to herself, "His sister? Diamond?"

"Yeah, I'm In—"

Before I can finish my sentence, the other bouncer who is with them steps up closer to me as if he wants to do something. Before taking another step, Big Sam 6'3", 280 pounds, former Golden Gloves heavyweight boxer who trained with DJ growing up, without hesitation rushes in quick and catches the dude with a right hook, knocking his ass out instantly. I can't help but to react, then landing a straight right to Cedric's face, breaking his nose. I continue throwing punches as the crew close in on him and the other two using bottles, chairs, and stomping. They pass out as much as they can. Dancers and patrons in the club start dispersing and getting out the way in panic from the melee that's taking place. I look around for Honey through all the shit that's going on but don't see her in the crowd. I am pissed that I'm not able to ask her about India now and her whereabouts.

Trying to make my way to the door, I see Dolo smack a guy unconscious trying to help the bouncers. Soon as he sees me, he grabs me and gets me out the club as fast as he can before the cops show up after being called. On our way through the door, DJ and the rest of the crew come running to the cars behind us. We do a head count to confirm and make sure everybody is present before we pull off. We peel out, all in the car, hyped up and laughing, talking shit about stomping on all them niggas for what they did to me the other day. I look back at the club parking lot full of people scattered everywhere running to their cars. I then see Delilah running out. She jumps into a blue Dodge Avenger. I made sure I get a real good look at her license plate too.

"I see you, HEK-5865, I'ma find yo ass now." We all quickly hit the highway back to Shaker Heights before any police even show up.

Chapter 12

Honey's Message (India's Story)

My eyes are closed, but my mind is racing. I'm stressing, contemplating my future, tossing, turning in this damn bed, trying my hardest to get comfortable and go to sleep. I'm surrounded by like eight or nine pillows, holding on to one of them, listening to my AC unit rattle and the sounds of the same infomercial on the TV playing again. If I know I am gonna have to suffer like this just to bring this little bad boy here, I will have changed my mind months ago. You probably heard of me by now. My name is India Williams, but you can call me Candice. Candice Law actually, a twenty-three-year-old divorced nurse's assistant from Pensacola, Florida.

I changed my name, changed my identity, left Raleigh, North Carolina, then came back home to Ohio with a close friend of mine, Delilah Stevens, about a year ago. Lilah is a few years older and just so happens to be from "The Land" just like me. My girl is a dance major, minoring in business. She is crazy as hell, outspoken, and a conscious sista. She protects me just like a big sister. After Dad died, it was just too much for me to handle alone, so she asked me to come back to Cleveland with her and reconnect with my family.

I want to get settled in first before calling anybody. I've only been here for a few months, plus I'm grown now, and this experience is different from when I was younger. I have money, so I don't need anything from anyone financially. Dad left me a nice chunk of change in his will, so I can do most of this by myself. I know Diamond and Mom are worried sick, not knowing and wondering where I could be, if I'm okay. It's been so long since we've seen one another that I'm kind of nervous for them to see me like this. Yes, I've deleted all my social network accounts so I can stay MIA from everyone, *everyone!* I know they're gonna have too many questions that I just don't want to answer right now, even to them. I am not settled mentally yet to talk to anybody.

Among other things, it's been extremely difficult dealing with not having Dad around anymore. He was all I knew. He was my best friend and my every day for the last ten years. It hurt my heart so bad watching him physically, spiritually, and mentally break down after the breakup with his fiancée because of the false accusations against him. In nine months, my father, the man who inspired me and taught me so much about what a man is, went from being a strong, handsome, social, independent charismatic gentleman to a depressed, bitter, drunken, chain-smoking, out-of-shape sluggish mess of what used to be a great man. I couldn't stand seeing him like that every day; I became depressed with him.

At first I was okay with juggling both high school and college, but when everything made headlines, I had to drop out of Blue Ridge and private school because of so many distractions. I was taking courses in business and computer information technologies so I can get my high school diploma and my associate's degree at the same time. Dad suggested that I finish my college career at an earlier age so I can have more years living, which I totally understand. After a few months of watching him let himself go, I just start staying with Delilah and her roommate or sometimes with my ex-boyfriend, Sean, who tried to be there for me as much as he could.

Sean Jones is the starting running back for the North Carolina Tar heels right now, but when we met, he was a redshirt freshman. He and I bumped into each other at a frat party Tiffany took me and Delilah to a year ago. He was cool at first, real laid-back, humble, and charming. We talked for a month or two before we got serious and became a couple. He was a few years older than me, a sophomore like Diamond, the pretty boy-type of ball player who loved the attention. He kept thinking it was okay to mess with all these girls on campus because I kept catching him, and I kept forgiving his cheating ass over and over again. His biggest problem was when the tables would turn and he would get jealous and mad when I was even around other males. He hated when I would have a good time with other men without him. I had to leave him alone though. I couldn't take his bullshit. He was egotistic, chauvinistic, insecure, and crazy. Whenever he was drinking, he would try to control me with his hands. He even tried it more than once, but as soon as I told Delilah that shit, she told the conscious brothas in her community organization about it. They approached him, and that shit never happened again. Right now that I'm back home and due, I can't afford to be around him or anybody with that type of energy. Shit, we can't afford it. Lilah knew how fragile and stressed I was becoming dealing with him and Dad's situation, and she wasn't having it. Even if I wanted to stay, the big sister in her made it her business to make me leave with her when she left. Sean only made my situation worse anyway even though I loved him a lot.

Tiffany Rothstein, the root of everything, played me and Dad for financial incentives from powers that be. Really to cover her own ass. As soon as word got out about her lies, the newspapers, the press, people at school, and even some of my closest friends and colleagues just turned on us without any real proof. This little rich dick-sucking white girl became my friend just to get close to my dad. She had his English Comp 1 and 2 class her freshman and sophomore year. He had a few one-on-one tutor sessions with her, and she claims to have fallen in love, infatuations really, with him since. So she starts hanging out with me and Delilah a lot just to be around him more. Can you believe that? At first we didn't care so much 'cause she had so much clout and money. Shopping would be on her a lot. We got into all the parties and clubs. We would hang out at their beach house in Daytona on spring break, skip classes, and still get credit for it. We kicked it with her. She knew her father didn't like that shit, but she did it anyway.

We both were daddy's girls, so we could relate in that aspect of friendship. She was just rich and wanted what she wanted; however, she had to get it because unlike my dad, her busy father never said no to her. Tiffany thought she had a chance at first when coming around, always trying to see what he was doing, all in his face flirting and wearing revealing clothes. Her dad was the dean, so she felt like she could do or say whatever she wanted to anybody, especially faculty.

Dad was single for years after him and Mom. He seen women on and off but never got too serious with any of them. Tiffany always felt like she had a chance, knowing that, but after months of pursuing Dad and being ignored, she backed off a little more. After a while, he began dating and getting serious with another faculty member who taught business there. Angela Owens, a Delta sorer. She was thirty-seven, divorced, no children, owned her home and two cars—2012 Jaguar and a 2014 Tahoe truck. She was high yellow just the way Dad likes them, extremely attractive, short, straight hair, solid body, not too thick but not skinny, with some big breast that Dad would gross me out talking about. Angie took a liking to me instantly, and I liked her too. She was that mother figure I felt I needed around for both of us since Mom was on the other side of the country in Arizona. Angie would help me with anything I needed; she would cook for us at the house or bring us food she would cook from home. Her and Dad would go out and do a variety of things, you know, like a couple looking to grow with one another would. Dinners, movies, plays, dancing, bowling, cruises, and even to the clubs sometimes. They dated about a year, and I could tell they were into each other. They soon got engaged and were gonna marry the next year. I was so happy for Dad and Angie.

Tiffany, on the other hand, didn't like their relationship at all and had other plans. Whenever she would come over after everyone knew their relationship was official, Tiff would always act real shitty toward Angie when she would see her, still flirty and extra. Even though she took Ms. Owens's algebra course a year ago and was a different kind of student to her then. Angie played it off as best as she could, but she still had her feeling about her, and Dad for some reason. I cussed Tiffany out for doing that shit, but being a spoiled bitch, she would do it anyway when she was into her feelings. All while the bitch was still fucking and sucking every athlete, Greek, or regular guy on campus. She was an attention whore with men she liked and hated being ignored, but my dad kept it business and professional with her at all times. She knew her father didn't like my father (because of his own personal reasons), so she went above and beyond just to be recognized in hopes of breaking him. The dean knew his little girl was out there, but he persuaded her to lie on Dad anyway just to get him fired. He hated the fact that his little girl wanted to be with black men so much.

* * *

One hot fall afternoon in 2012, Delilah and Tiffany came through to hang out with me after class to prepare and plan for the Drake concert coming to town in the next few weeks. We were all sitting in my room listening to music, watching TV, and even doing some online shopping—on Tiffany again. I could hear Dad pulling in the driveway at his normal time of 4:38 every day, bumping his Tupac, whom he played on the regular. After he walked in the door and came upstairs, he heard Chris Brown playing loud and clear, so he knocked on my door first to let me know he was home.

"Knock knock!"

I say, "Come in!"

"Hey, Indy, I'm home. How y'all girls doings?"

"Hey, Dad!"

Delilah says, "Hey, Mr. Williams."

Tiffany says, "Hi, Emmanuel."

"I'm about to get clean real quick and finish grading some papers. Y'all hungry? Y'all want me to order some food?"

Tiffany said, "I want something to eat."

"Girl, naw, we okay for now, Dad. We're gonna pick up something later when we go out. Thank you though. Love you!"

"Love you too, baby. You young ladies have fun. I'll be in my room if you need me."

He closed the door and went to do what he do to wind down for the day. About ten minutes or so later, Tiffany decided that she had to go to her car, so she excused herself. She was gone, I say, for about fifteen to twenty minutes, but when she came back to my room, she told us she had to leave. Her clothes were hanging off, and she had a frantic look in her eyes. She immediately grabbed her things in a hurry and just left. We asked her if something wrong, but she didn't say anything to us. She just walked out the door. At the time, I really wasn't thinking of anything because all of us were just having a good time. I mean, we thought it could have been her time of the month or she got a phone call about some dude playing her again, or the bitch could have been pregnant. But anyway, that night, my father never came out of his room though. I thought it was unusual because he always said good night to me before we both went to bed even if Angela was over, but he never did that night. That next morning, around 7:15 a.m. while I was in the bathroom finishing up on my hair getting ready for school and Dad was in his room getting ready for work, we heard a loud banging on the door. We both rushed to the front door to see who it was knocking like the po-po, only to arrive at the door to be greeted by two police officers.

Emmanuel says, "Good morning, officers. How can I help you?"

"Are you Emmanuel Williams?"

"Yes, sir, I am. What's going on?"

"Sir, we have a warrant for your arrest. You're being charged with sexual assault, and you're gonna have to come with us?

I say, "What are y'all talking about? Dad! What's going on?"

"Hold on. Hold on. You mean to tell me that she said I assaulted her? What the fuck! I didn't touch that girl! She came on to me!"

"Turn around, sir. You have the right to remain silent. Anything you say and do may count against you in a court of law. You have the right to etc—"

"What girl? Dad, who is he talking about?"

"She set me up, India, I swear! Call my lawyer."

They quickly read him his rights, handed me a copy of the warrant, put him in cuffs, and then walked him to the police cruiser. That bitch Tiffany actually sat in my face being a friend to me all this time, then turned around and accused my father of raping her yesterday when she left my room to go the bathroom. I couldn't believe this girl. Once I contacted his lawyer, we was able to bail him out on bond later on that day. When I picked him up from the station, it was a very quiet ride back home. Dad was so distraught over the situation he just couldn't come to say a word to me, and honestly, I didn't know what to say to him either. We got to the house, and he immediately went to his bedroom and got in the shower. He stayed in his room for about an hour, then came out in the kitchen where I was cooking us dinner. He sat down at the kitchen table with his head down and pain in his voice to tell me that his and Angie's relationship was over and that she wouldn't even talk to him or answer his phone calls right now. He then looked me in my eyes and explained to me what really happened yesterday with Tiffany. He said she knocked on his door right after he got out the shower.

My cell phone starts ringing. "Hold up. Let me answer this."

Chapter 13

He's Looking for You

THIS GIRL KNOWS I got to get up in the morning. Why is she calling me so late?

I answer, "What's up, girl? what you calling me at? What time is it? 2:53 in the morning for?"

Delilah replies, "Girl! It's just went down at the bar tonight. It was a fucking brawl!"

"Damn! Who? What? Was it people at the club or the security fighting?"

"Everybody in the gotdamn club was fighting. It was crazy!"

"You wasn't fighting, was you?"

"Naw, girl, but I had to duck a few punches and bottles. I'm good, though. I got my black ass right out the way back to my locker to get my shit and go."

"Well, what happened?"

"Okay, remember the other day when I called you and told you my brothers fucked some dude up who was at the club asking about you and me."

"Yeah, I remember. Was it him?"

"Well, I wasn't there to see who he was that night. My brothers didn't really tell me what he looked like. They just figured he was your ex because he was asking about both of us, telling them he knew us from North Carolina. Cordell immediately got mad 'cause he figured it was him, then went and got Cedric. Girl, they came back and confronted him, then before he could say or do anything else, they roughed him up."

"Okay…"

"Found out tonight that was not Sean."

"It wasn't?"

"*No!* Tonight at the club, I knew I had seen him before. I just couldn't figure it out until it was too late. I was about to give him a dance and everything with his fine ass."

"Bitch! If it wasn't Sean, then who are you talking about?"

"Girl, that was your brother, Diamond! He was there looking for you again. He was with this group of like fifteen or twenty people this time all dressed in black, females too, ready to fuck some shit up!"

"What!"

Heart racing, even more shocked that Diamond has left school in California to come and find me here to Ohio. Knowing he must have been to North Carolina and know about Dad now. Shit!

"Did you get to talk to him at all?"

"I did for a short minute. He told me his name was D, but at the time, I didn't put that together or even ask his whole name. We was flirting with each other too 'cause he was trying to get a dance from me. I went to the bar to get a drink, then my brothers saw him, approached him. His people got up, and everything went down from there. I still got his fifty dollars too. I ain't gone lie, girl. They spent some money while they was in there, but when shit went down, they wasn't playing! For real, though, they fucked some shit up. Some of the dudes with him was bigger than some of our bouncers."

"Oh my god! I can't believe they did that to my brother, thinking he was Sean."

"Yeah, girl, they say they put him in the hospital."

"Damn, I know I got to call my brother now. I'm thinking I'm doing everybody a favor by staying away, and my brother end up getting hurt looking for me. I feel like that was my fault. The problem is, if he was that deep in the club the second time he showed up, he was most likely with my cousin DJ, and that's not good at all."

"What you mean not good at all?"

"This situation is just getting started with them. To fuckin' steal money from him or my aunt and uncle is crazy, but to hurt or kill somebody in our family is suicide. Here in Cleveland, my cousin DJ is a dangerous individual, just like his father was. They don't play. They're vicious. They have the money, the power, and the respect around town to do a lot of things to a lot of people if they cross them. They will find me sooner than later. I know your brothers are big, but they got more people, money, and resources. They will kill family members and anybody else to find me and for doing what your brothers did to Diamond. If my brother is trying to find me here in Cleveland, I know my mother is on her way here too."

"What you gon' do, girl? What do I do? I need to know what I gotta watch out for now?"

"I'll call you, or you call me in the morning. I got to make some phone calls now."

"Okay, you tell your fine-ass brother to call me when you finally talk to him."

"Girl, please you just be careful out there and text me when you get home."

"Okay, I will. I didn't mean to startle you either, girl. How you feeling, and how's my god son little D doing?"

"Girl, he keep kicking me. I know he gon' be bad. I can tell already, but I'm fine. Just waiting till his little butt get here. Well, let me try to go back to sleep 'cause I know I need to talk to some family now. I got to go to the hospital in the morning too."

"All right, girl. You let me know what's going on, and I'll do the same."

"Okay, Lilah. Love you, girl. Thank you for everything."

"Love you too, Dia, sisters for life. Call you tomorrow. Bye."

"Bye."

I hang up the phone in shock. I know the day will come when Diamond is going to show up wherever I am, looking for me. I just don't know it will be this soon. My big brother, boy, does he hate the fact that we are broken apart because of our parents' issues with each other. He used to always say to me all the time before the divorce,

"Sis, we can go live with Nana and Pops, and Mom and Dad can move away by the self, leave us here." That isn't happening though.

I'm so scared for Diamond to see me. I know how overprotective he has always been, so to see me like this now, he will be disappointed, especially with me dropping out of school. I know with him still being in college, he expects for me to be in school too. Our parents and their parents instilled in us to finish school no matter what. I promise myself I will as soon as I can. Before I came back to Cleveland, I reached out to a close family member and told her I was coming back home, but I made her promise to keep my presence here a secret until I told her to, even from my mother and from Diamond. My favorite person and my guide through this journey. My Nana, Hope Wadsworth-Meyers. She will be going with me to the hospital in the morning. I know it's gonna be even harder to sleep now with this new information about my brother and what happened to him trying to find me. I got to get my rest for now though, for me and my little man, so let me just close my eyes, breathe, relax, and focus on handling everything I need to handle tomorrow.

Me and Nana's Promise

Boom, boom, boom, boom, boom, boom!

In something like a coma while deep into a crazy dream about my mom, dad, and Diamond, I instantly wake up almost in panic to the sound of loud knocking at my front door. I look at the clock, and it's 8:45 a.m. I overslept. Knocking this hard, I know she must be mad at me. I pick up my phone to see that she's been calling me too, uh ooh. Let me get up. I slowly roll over to get up out of the bed, grab and put on my housecoat, then go get the door. I open up, yawning, still sleepy as she walks right in, screaming at me.

"Girl, I been calling you all morning. Done got my blood pressure all up, worrying and thinking that boy done found you with nobody here to help you. Girl, I had to bring my 9 for protection."

"Really, Nana?"

"You damn right. So pick up the phone when you see me calling, you hear me"—*heavy breathing*—"are you okay?"

"Yeah, I'm okay, and I'm so sorry I was knocked out. I didn't hear anything, and this boy keeps me tired."

Just like Nana, bringing the Blackfoot out, face red, head full of long silver natural hair, done up in a ponytail, still pretty. But when she is upset, she is as bossy, fussy, prepared, crazy, mad, and all that. Even though I know at the end of the day, she is just concerned about me. In her own unique way. The sun is out, so she dressed all fly today. Got her sunglasses on, a gray-and-blue casual sweat suit on, and to make it so bad, she got the nerve to have on some gray Air Force 1s. That's my Nana though, styling still at the age of sixty-four years young.

"Yes, ma'am."

"You gon' head hurry up and get dressed. We gotta make your appointment, Dinah."

"Yes, ma'am, okay, but can you come help me, please?"

"Come on."

She follows me as I waddle back to my room, continuing our conversation. While she's helping me get dressed, I just can't hold it in any longer on what's been hurting me since last year up until all last night.

"Guess what? Delilah called me at like three in the morning with some crazy news."

"What you hear?"

"I just found out that Diamond is here looking for me."

"I know, baby?"

"You do? Well, I heard Diamond has been here for a couple of days."

"Your Aunt Debbie told me he's here looking for you."

"I'm so sorry, Nana. Those were Delilah's brothers that did that to him. They thought he was Sean, and they know about him putting his hands on me. I didn't think Diamond's gonna go there even if he was looking for me."

"It's fine, baby. You can apologize to him when you see him again. I'm happy Lila's brother is looking out for you for that, and you're right, they just didn't know. Your mother is supposed to come and see me tomorrow though. It's perfect timing too, you think?"

"I wouldn't say that. Did you tell them about me?"

"No, I didn't, even though that's my daughter, and I know she's worried sick about you. I made you a promise, Diah. Your brother, though, he is going through hell and high water to find you. You know how he is, just like your father, rest his soul, when it comes to you."

"I know, I know. He went to Delilah's job last night at Club Secrets with DJ looking for me again. She said they tore up the club because of what they did to him from the last time he was there."

"Yeah, your Aunt Debbie and DJ picked him up from the hospital. He left school, practice, and sacrificed everything he had going on to come here and find you. His crazy self randomly came here without even letting any of us know he was here until after the fact, just like you. And when it comes to DJ, my grandson is what he is. We all know how they can be."

"I know. I got to talk to him sooner than later."

"Yes, you do, before things get worst."

I finished putting on my last bit of lip gloss in the mirror and slip into my white sandals to match this white maternity sundress to fit my big belly.

"Okay, Nana. I'm ready."

We both come from out of my bedroom into the living room area, ready to leave. I'm hungry, but I feel stuffed. All this extra weight I gained I can barely fit into even my maternity clothes. Two more weeks and Diamond Emmanuel Williams will be here, and I can tell now that this boy gon' be big.

"Look at your big self, girl. If and when your mother see you, she would still be proud of you, baby girl. You are intelligent, beautiful, responsible, and a loving young black goddess. You are doing a fantastic job handling all of this like you is."

"Thank you, Nana. This is hard, very very hard dealing with Dad being gone and now having a baby. It hurts being alone so much. I know I wouldn't have been able to get through these hard times without you and Delilah being there for me."

I grab my purse from off the stand next to the door, and we both head outside. I lock the door behind me, then we walk out to the car parked in a handicap spot out front. She grabs her keys, then hits the buttons to unlock the door to her brand-new sky-blue 2014 Chevy Malibu. After North Carolina, I decided to move to Twinsburg instead of back in the heart of Cleveland like before because I really didn't want to run into anybody I didn't want to see. I'm living comfortably and out the way in my two-bedroom first-floor luxury apartment on Pebble Creek Drive. Nana don't mind coming out to see me from Shaker. We always have fun together because it's a lot of shopping to do around where I stay. She helps me inside the car, and we head out to the Twinsburg Cleveland Clinic facility where my physician, Dr. Rebecca Boley, is patiently waiting on me.

* * *

I spend about half an hour in the doctor's office, fifteen minutes waiting and fifteen minutes checking my blood pressure, my weight, his frequent movements, urine samples, measuring my womb, and checking my dilations, assuring he is ready to meet his momma. I'm also making arrangements, preparing for this due date, which could be any day now. Dr. Boley has been a doll, nurturing me along with Lilah and Nana, always going above and beyond her doctor duties to help me through this situation. She knows about my journey back home, about Dad, Diamond, and my solo lifestyle here in Twinsburg. She also knows that his father, Sean, isn't here going through this with me. I'm only a few weeks away, and she's concerned about where I'll be and who I'll be with when the contractions increase and my water breaks. I do have Nana (*who's in the room with me sitting in the chair, waiting*), but because I haven't been in contact with any other family in Cleveland, Dr.—or Rebecca as a friend—made me put her personal cell number in my phone and keep it on speed dial whenever I need her. Her husband, Mark, is an architect who works from home, so he helps with their three children to where she can come and go when needed, doctor on call.

"Okay, Diah, you're all set. So…are you excited?"

"I am, but I'm tired, and he need to get here soon. My feet hurt, and I don't want to carry all this weight around with me no more."

"Yeah, I've been there three times. As beautiful and as much of a blessing all my babies were, going through each pregnancy was different, but all of them was something else."

Nana says, "I know that, and I did it back in the old days when we didn't have all that medicine these young girls got now. Girl, you talking about going through it, don't get me started."

"Yes, I know, Mrs. Meyers. You're right. It was harder for you ladies back then, more pain."

I finish putting my clothes on. We share a hug, then all walk out into the hallway. Rebecca walks with us on our way to the elevator

"Well, Doc, I will see you in a few weeks or sooner to deliver this boy. Thank you so much. I appreciate everything you're doing for me."

"You know it's nothing, Liah. You just better call me and keep me posted on your condition day-to-day, okay?"

"Yes, ma'am, I will."

"I'll be by her side as much as I can, making sure she's looked after, Doctor."

"Okay, bye, ladies."

"Bye."

"All right now."

Nana and I make our way back to the car, now debating on what we want for breakfast this morning. We head in the direction of the Cracker Barrel and Bob Evens so we can decide which of the two to eat. After that, we then plan on heading to the shopping plaza close by so we can pick up a few things afterward for ourselves and Lil D (*even though he has everything he needs*). Nana and I really like hanging out together. We do it so we can bond and make up some of the lost time we missed with each other over the years. We get to her ride, and she helps my fat self get in the car again. She shuts the door, walks around to get in, starts the car, and we head out. While we're riding to our destination, I get to thinking, and out of the blue, my emotions elevate instantly, feeling so bad about how I am always talking or thinking about my situation and never asking Nana about her situation. Thinking about how she has been managing her own situation, dealing with losing Papa just two years ago to colon cancer. Every day, she still finds a way to help me as much as she does. So I take a moment and ask her.

"You miss Papa, Nana?"

She pauses for a moment, looks at me, then continues to drive.

"Every minute of the day, baby. I never thought it would be this hard living life without him. He is all over that house. I feel him in the bedroom, in the living room watching TV, in the kitchen, waiting on me to make his plate, everywhere. After forty years, I feel I don't have a reason to cook. I don't have a reason to clean up after anyone, and now I don't have a reason to even be at home...alone. To be honest, you coming here has really helped me. That's why I offer to help you this much."

"Awww, Nana." I am tearing up.

"You're about to bring me another great-grandbaby in this world, Diah, giving me a great reason to love again as much as I loved your grandfather. The Lord knew I couldn't do this by myself either, Diah."

"I understand that now. Dad was just there for me so much. He always handled everything. I felt like I could do it alone too even if I didn't want to."

"Well, you don't have to because I'm here."

"And I'm here for you too, Nana. We can do this together. Next questions, do you talk to Auntie Debbie or Auntie Audrey often?"

"Well, I talk to Debbie all the time. She come over the house at least once a week, but me and your Auntie Audrey aren't on good terms right now."

"Why not? I mean, I thought she was cool. She seemed different to me than Mom or Aunt Debbie 'cause she was quiet. Always in her room when we would come by back in the day."

"Well, Diah, I can take blame for the reasons she was that way. Just know even your Nana ain't perfect, baby. I have my own faults and some of my own secrets that I'm dealing with."

"What do you mean?"

"Audi was always a calm and mellow child. Even as a baby, she really didn't cry. She would just look at you. When she got older, she never wanted much but to keep learning. I don't know if she was quiet because her sisters got so much attention or what. I mean, Debbie and your mother got good grades. We made sure of that, but they were just girly girls. Always wanted their hair done, always having new clothes if we bought them or they did, and boys was always calling the house for them. Especially that Debbie and Derek with his craziness. Audrey never cared about any of that though."

"Yeah, my dad told me he used to call a lot, and y'all used to cuss him out for calling so late."

"I didn't want none of them little fast boys around my girls, so yeah, me and your grandfather cursed them all out for calling."

"You crazy, Nana!"

"Yeah, I am, but with Audi, she was just like you said—different. But I never really had a problem with it. Diah, Nana got something to tell you, and I need you to keep this between you and me."

"Okay?"

"After your mother was born, for a few years, me and your grandfather's relationship was on the rocks. We were actually on the brink of divorce for many reasons, mine and his. His lack of presence at home with me raising the girls all by myself became a problem. I went back to work after my twelve weeks of having your mother because we still had bills to pay, and I just couldn't sit at home no more. Because their father never had any spare time, I had to leave the girls over our next-door neighbors Ms. Cunningham's house while we were both at work throughout the week. I later found out from one of his buddies he claim to be hanging out with all the time that he had been having an affair with one of his coworkers for a while. After the first year of knowing, I didn't say nothing even after all I knew. I just let it go on for another year, and then I eventually checked him on it."

"So you let him cheat for a whole year before you said something? Why?"

"Well, Diah, we were young when we got together. We went to grade school together and high school together, even went to the same college in love. So by the time we were married with two children, I knew he felt trapped. And like him, I wanted something different too, so I did. What pissed me off the most, though, is how I felt when he looked me and my daughters in our faces every day and lied to us, knowing he was going to see her. It hurt like hell, and I've always loved my girls and your grandfather, but I did not want him to have all the fun. So I did me for me that next year."

"Nana! I know you didn't on Grandpa? With who?"

"No, I did not cheat on your grandfather. We were playing the same game. I wasn't gonna be the type of woman to be crying and asking why and complaining about what he got to lose at home and all that weak woman shit. I made sure I enjoyed my playtime just like he enjoyed his. His name was Morris Washington. He was a guy I went to high school with from around my old neighborhood. We ran into each other while I was out shopping with the girls one day after I found out about your grandfather. At that time, Morris was in the Marine Corps and was home for a while until he shipped back out overseas. He was a gorgeous peanut butter complexion brother and a gentleman in every way. He never judged me or my husband in our situation. He let me vent as long as I wanted about whatever I wanted to. Morris always looked at me and made me feel beautiful. He always touched me and held me the way I needed him to and when I needed him to. He was just a little bit taller than me, a real nice toned body from training, and girl was he packing. I mean, damn!"

"Ewe, Nana. I don't want to hear that. I can't believe you being a nasty butt."

"Hey, girl, you gon' learn one day men ain't the only ones who can do they thing."

Flowing through traffic on our way to our destination, we finally arrive at the Cracker Barrel off Aurora Road. We find an open space in the crowded lot, park the car, and sit for a minute, continuing our conversation.

"Karma to me having my fun is and my regrets are when I told him I knew about him and his infidelities, I then told him about what I was doing. My problem was by that time, I was pregnant with your Auntie Audrey."

"So you…you trying to tell me… Nana, you trying to tell me that Auntie Audrey ain't Grandpa's?"

"What I'm telling you, India, is, your Auntie Audrey is not your grandfather's daughter."

"Oh my god! Does he know? Did he know then?"

"Yes, I sat him down and told him right after I found out. I looked him in his eyes and spoke the truth. I told him about everything I knew he had been doing over the years. About everything I had done and what has come about to me reacting to his lies and me being reckless and having my own fun. You see, Diah, your grandfather and Pam Jones end up having a son on us, a little boy named Sherman Jr. Yes, you have an uncle that lives in Detroit now. He's a year younger than your mother. I met him for the first time at your grandfather's funeral. Your Pops had been back and forth with home and living with his second family across town. Believe me, Diah, I had worst intentions than what I did when I first found out about this. It broke my heart in every possible way. I didn't know how to feel about my pregnancy at first. I knew what I was doing was wrong, but honestly, I wanted him to feel my pain. I just didn't know how Morris was gonna take it. After he shipped out while I was seven months pregnant, I never heard from or seen him again. When Audrey was five years old, I ran into his brother, and he told me that he was killed in the war.

"Wow, Nana, that's crazy."

"When I told your grandfather about me and Morris and that the baby could possibly be his, I told him he could either stay and deal with both of our wrongs, or he can leave, and I can raise my three girls alone. He was hurt, really hurt, and even threatened to leave, but when he realized he was the cause and this was the effect of everything, he decided to cut off his ties with Pam, still provide for Sherman Jr., but remain a man to his immediate family. Although she tried to keep him from his son because of that, your grandfather knew we're more important to lose. We forgave each other and remained faithful since. Even though he knew she was not his daughter, he still loved Audrey the same and, in some cases, gave her more time and attention than Debbie and your mother. I always thought it was a reflection of our—his and my—mistakes. I actually fought up enough nerve and told Audrey about everything right after your grandfather died."

"What she say?

"She didn't want to believe me at first, but something deep down in her knew she was always different. After I told her what transpired from me and your Pop's infidelities, she hung up the phone, angry at us for not telling her sooner. She hasn't answered any of me and her sisters' calls since until this morning. I told her about what's going on right now with this family, and she called me back. We talked, and she wants her sisters to know. They don't know yet, but I'm going to tell them both when your mother comes in. You're gonna have to talk to your mother and your brother also, Diah. These secrets hurt not only others but yourself."

"You right, Nana. How do we do it?"

"I have a plan. Let's go eat, and I'll tell you."

"Cool. Let's go."

We get out the car and walk inside the restaurant and enjoy our brunch together.

Chapter 15

Nostalgia Has Arrived

"Excuse me."

"Yes, ma'am."

"Can I have another rum and Coke, please?"

"No problem, ma'am. I'll be right back."

"Thank you."

The young, spunky, and helpful attendant, Telisha, smiles and walks in the back to prepare me another round. I am enjoying this moment all to myself, relaxing. No meetings, no clients, colleagues, nothing. Just peace and quiet sitting comfortable in my first-class seat, slowly intensifying a buzz I feel coming on. I just finished a chapter of one of my favorite books *Dutch II: Angel's Revenge* by Teri Woods while waiting on my fourth Cuba Libre. I'm on a flight about to touch down back in Cleveland, Ohio. Shit, I fly Delta throughout the year for work so much that I've earned enough mileage points to pay for this trip.

I guess I'm drinking right now to help me cope with these unstable emotions I have, thinking about how hard it must be for Diamond and India being back home and dealing with losing their father. Our family started here, and it is just filled with so many memories, good and bad. As I finish my last sip of my third drink, out comes the friendly and helpful flight attendant Telisha with empty hands:

"I'm sorry, ma'am, but I've been informed we're not serving any more drinks right now only because we are about to land."

"Dang, I wanted that drink too, man, okay."

"I'm so sorry."

"I'm just teasing you. Thank you."

She smiles, walks away, then grabs the horn and makes an announcement.

"Ladies and gentlemen, welcome to Cleveland Hopkins Airport. The local time is 3:28 p.m., and the temperature is eighty-four degrees.

"For your safety and comfort, please remain seated with your seat belt fastened until the captain turns off the Fasten Seat Belt sign. This will indicate that we have parked at the gate and that it is safe for you to move about. At this time, you may use your cellular phones if you wish. Cellular phones may only be used once the Fasten Seat Belt sign has been turned off.

"Please check around your seat for any personal belongings you may have brought on board with you, and please use caution when opening overhead bins as heavy articles may have shifted around during the flight.

"If you require deplaning assistance, please remain in your seat until all other passengers have deplaned. One of our crew member will then be pleased to assist you.

"On behalf of Delta Airlines and the entire crew, I'd like to thank you for joining us on this trip, and we are looking forward to seeing you on board again in the near future. Have a nice day."

* * *

Excited, nervous, but not much in a hurry, I get up out of my seat first just to stretch from me sitting for so long. I then *inhale and exhale*, take a deep breath, and prepare myself before reconnecting with Momma, my sisters, Diamond, and the rest of my loved ones back here in Cleveland, Ohio. Hoping we can find my baby India while we all here too. I reach in the overhead bin to grab my laptop bag and gather the few items I brought on board with me. I follow the slow-moving line of passengers off the plane and through the tunnel. Debbie knew to pick me up at 3:30. It's 3:36 now, so I hope that she is here already. While waiting five minutes or so in baggage claim for my luggage, I see her crazy self walking in the door looking like a thicker, darker version of me. Ghetto fabulous as always, hair sharp, draped in red with the heels and glasses, making an entrance, yelling my nickname all loud for everybody to hear.

Debbie shouts, "*Eve!* Ah, ah, ah! *Eve!* Eveee! Hey, sis!"

"Heeeeeey, Debbi, *or ah!* What's up, girl?"

We both run over, jumping up and down to embrace each other.

"It's so good to see you again, sis."

"You too, girl. It's been too long since Dad's funeral, right?"

"Yeah, it has been, about a year or two. I'm sorry you gotta be back here again under these circumstances, though."

"It's okay, really. It's kind of like life telling me I need to come home more. Part of me has always felt like I ran away from my issues years ago when me and Emmanuel separated. I guess this is the opportunity for me to face everything I didn't face back then while I'm here, this time."

"Eve it's, all good. Just like we told Diamond, we got you. I know you've been busy living that fast life out on the West Coast, making moves and selling properties left and right, I hear."

"Well, you know [*shrugging and popping my collar*], I do what I can do when I can do it. And what I can do is get that money, baby!"

"You damn right. That's how we all roll. You ready to go, let you see how I do what I do round these parts."

"I see you with that new Michael Kors purse."

"Girl, this just one of 'em. Come on. Let me show you my new baby."

"New baby, huh?"

She takes one of my bags of Louis Vuitton luggage for me; I follow her as we head outside to her car. Smiling at me the whole time, she hits the button to unlock the door of her candy-apple-red 2014 Benz truck that matches her red ensemble.

"Bitch, no, you didn't! Okay, okay, I see you working hard too, huh?"

"You damn right. So where you wanna go first, check in your room or check on Momma?"

"You talk to her?"

"Naw, I just got off work. I ain't get a chance to call her. I been dealing with a family reunion all week at the hotel, but you can call her."

"Yeah, I'm about to, but we can go ahead and head to the room. I'm a call Diamond's crazy self to see if he heard anything about India."

"When the last time you talked to him?"

"We texted the other day, but I ain't talked to him in a couple of days."

"Hmm!"

"What?"

"Well, DJ told me they had a pretty interesting night the other day trying to find her, but you can call him. He'll tell you."

"Really! What happened? Let me call him."

We finish loading my luggage in her brand-new Mercedes, get in the car, and head 480 East to 77 North on our way to her hotel downtown. I grab my phone from out my purse and call this boy to find out what Debbie is talking about.

The phone rings and keeps on ringing…voice mail comes on. I leave him a message.

"Diamond, this is your mother. I'm in Cleveland now about to go check into the hotel, so hit me back when you get this message. I want to know if you found out anything about your sister, and I hope you're staying safe doing so. Call me. Bye."

I hang up the phone and text him to get back to me ASAP.

"He ain't answer. Debbie, what is going on?"

"I wanted him to tell you 'cause I ain't got nothing to do with any of it. All I can tell you is they're doing what they have to do to get some information on your daughter."

"[*Angry and impatient*] Girl, what the hell happen?"

"All right, all right! Well, you know he got jumped by some bouncers at the strip club he went to when he got here looking for India."

"Yeah, I heard."

"You called us, we called him, then we picked him up from the hospital. Once he told us what happen and you know how we get down, DJ got some of his crew together with Diamond, and they went back to the club to find out what they knew."

"So what happened?"

"They tore that bitch up! It was all on the news and everything, but everybody in crew got out."

"So is he all right? Did he get hurt or do anything that will fuck up him playing next season?"

"Naw, girl, I told you they all good. They took care of business and got out. We won't put him in a situation that would mess up his basketball career."

"This is too much. I need a drink."

"They good, you good, so we good, lil sis. We ain't in Arizona, girl. Shit goes down here in the land. You out of all people by now should know what we do and how we do it. Ain't no fucking games here. You touch one of ours, you gon' have to deal with the conse-quences of your actions, period! We don't do that court shit. Them was some hood niggas that did that to Diamond, and they could have ruined his basketball career! Around here, we do hood shit back. Just know that only because of y'all, we didn't do more and shoot that bitch up. People around here know Diamond is our family. We got a reputation to protect."

Shocked by her outburst and instant mood change, I pause for a minute before I respond.

"Damn, girl, I hear you. I'm just concerned with my son and my daughter's well-being right now. You ain't gotta get all gangsta on a bitch. Damn!"

"My bad, baby sis. It's just this lifestyle can get to me. It's serious and cutthroat, especially being a woman running it. I can't and won't show any mercy on anybody for any reason. The moment I show weakness out here, somebody a take me out or try to set me up like they did my husband. Even though Derek keeps me protected on these streets, I got men that will die for me out here, sis. If anybody wanna get cute if I'm out here solo, shit, I stay strapped my damn self."

She pulls out a Heckler and Kotch nickel-plated 9 millimeter from out her red Michael Kors purse to let me know she's ready for whatever.

"Got my CCWs, so I'm licensed to carry, and I made sure I picked up some extra insurance on every end for myself and the kids just in case something was to happen."

"I hear you. I need one of them too. Protection is a must."

"If you need one, I can send one out to you."

"I'll take it. Just send it. I can get my CCWs soon as I get back. I want you to know, too, that you can always call me with the kids. Y'all can come and stay with me out in Scottsdale anytime. I am just as much here for you and yours like you are for me and mine. I love y'all."

"We love you too. Hey! I got an idea. You should let me treat you to a signature full-body massage, a manicure, and a citrus pedicure. Get you relaxed a little bit before we go to check in the hotel. We got time."

"That's fine with me. I don't mind at all, but you gotta let me pay, though. You're doing all this for us—the room, helping me with Diamond and India. Debbie, I can foot the bill on something if you let me. Just to show you my appreciation, you know."

"Not happening, sis. You back home, which is my city now. Don't insult me like that. I got this."

"Well, I ain't never had a problem with free, and I won't ask you again. Let's go then."

She touches the phone button in her car and makes a call to her favorite place, Marengo Luxury Spa downtown on Euclid. She scheduled our appointment for "The Great Escape" package, which includes an aromatherapy full-body massage and a deep cleansing facial. Appointment set, so now we are on our way to get pampered.

"I ain't gon' lie. I was not expecting this, but I can say this is a great start to my trip so far."

"Girl, while you here this time, we gon' have some fun. We might just get into some trouble too."

"Ahh hhn, I ain't messing with you."

"We a see. We still gotta find India, remember? We a do what we gotta do to find her, right?"

"Yeah, well, we gon' take the right approach first, sis, okay?"

"Okay, but if that shit don't work, we doing it my way."

En route to downtown Cleveland, the nostalgia being back in the land kicks in. Got me enjoying the Midwest vibe again, the *Beacon Journal*, the Cleveland Clinic, the Steelyards, the Browns Stadium, the now Progressive Field and the Cavs with Quicken Loans Arena. The Horseshoe, baby. We got a casino now? It's home in many ways, but at the same time, home has changed a lot. Except for these empty-ass broken-down houses and the same fucked-up roads. I'm just getting back, so I don't know if I like it or not. I just need to find my baby, and then I'll know.

We eventually arrive at Marengo's around 4:15 p.m. We walk into a cool welcoming lobby, greeted by the owner and close friend of Debbie's, Darlene Rubertino. A Florida native but Italian in every way, Darlene is a forty-year-old former swimsuit model, wife, and mother of two. She moved to Ohio about five years ago, invested most of her modeling money into her business, and has been a successful entrepreneur ever since. She welcomes us at the door with smiles, hugs, and tall glasses of fresh cucumber water. She and the few staff members who will be servicing us today escort us to our lockers to change our clothes and get prepared.

We spend the next hour and a forty-five minutes getting relaxed, revitalized, exfoliated, and rejuvenated. Debbie and Darlene have a mutual agreement and understanding with business beyond this spa or the hotel, so she gave us a few extra hours to do us. Once the other clients leave and they close for the day, we spend the rest of our personal time reclined in our seats, enjoying our pedicure treatments first, to the sound of atmospheric sounds and soft jazz. I am in the relaxation room with my big sister doing just that—relaxing, drinking on champagne, eating cheese, crackers, chocolate, fruit, and chocolate-covered fruit. I'm letting my feet soak before April starts with the pumice stone. My phone rings.

"Took long enough."

"Is it him?"

"Yeah, it's him."

Diamond is calling.

"Hello!"

Diamond replies, "What's up, Ma?"

"Boy, where the hell are you at? And what is this I'm hearing about shit you doing being all on the news and shit?"

"Damn, Ma. how you doing? I'm fine, by the way. Everything is all good. We got a lead when we went to the club the other night. We checking on India's friend Delilah now. I can tell she know something. It's just when I was about to talk to her, we got into it with the same dudes that jumped me when I got here, her brothers. We gon' find her. I seen her car. I know what she drive, and I got her license plate. When we get that info, we can go talk to her about sis."

"Okay, that's good to hear. You talk to your grandmother yet?"

"Naw, but I called her and left a message. I was really waiting till you got here to go see her."

"Okay, we can go see her tomorrow or sometime this week while I'm here."

"Cool, I'm over a friend's house right now, though, a young lady DJ and his girl introduced me to when I got here. Her name is Brittany. She the one who actually help me find out some stuff about India's friend. I want you to meet her."

"You want me to meet her, huh? Well, tell Ms. Brittany that I said thank you for helping us. I'm with your aunt right now getting pampered at the spa. I'ma call you when I get checked in the hotel. You going back to your room tonight?"

"I might. I'll let you know. For now, I'm chilling, laying low with Brittany. And tell Auntie I said hey. Let her know that DJ is with his girl, well, 'fiancée, and Faith. We are staying out the way too, Momma, so don't worry."

"Don't make me worry coming out here doing all this crazy stuff. You know I ain't ready for all this, Diamond."

"I know you not, Ma. I'm not either. I'm just trying to find sis."

We will. We will. You be careful out there. Luv you."

"Luv you too, peace."

"Bye."

I take a deep sigh and hang up the phone with a since of relief knowing that he's somewhere out the way and not into any trouble. I can get fully into my relaxing now.

Debbie says, "I told you they good, girl."

"Yeah, he told me they laying low. DJ is over his girlfriend's or his fiancée's house with their daughter. I didn't know he was getting married?"

"He proposed to her about a month ago right after she graduated from Cleveland State with her bachelor's. They planning for the wedding to be next year around August, I think. He was so sweet surprising her at her graduation party with a two-carat round-cut diamond ring, had her friends gawking like a muhfucka."

"Go 'head, DJ."

"That boy maybe crazy, hood, and gangsta just like his daddy, but he keep a soft spot for Nora and Faith, spoiling them every chance he get."

"I know that. Diamond told me that DJ's girl hooked him up with one of her friends, some girl named Brittany."

"Oh, okay, I like her. Brittany is a sweet young lady. She was going to school with DJ's girl. She a be good for Diamond. I know he like her."

"Why you say that?"

"She thick, chocolate, pretty, and rock her own hair. I don't know about how the girls are in Arizona or LA, but she is a catch for any man anywhere."

"Well, I can't wait to meet her then. You and him got me convinced she's a nice young lady. Now let me catch up with you. Girl, pour me some more of that champagne. I'm feeling good now."

"I told you everything was gon' be all right. We ain't got nothing to worry about. Here you go. Uh-oh."

Debbie, myself, and Darlene, who decided to join us with our manicures, have been vibing, drinking, and passing the time. After pouring the last to fill up my glass, we noticed that we've went through three bottles of Dom Pérignon. The party is just getting started, and we are cranked up.

"Hey, Darlene!"

"What's up, girl?"

"Can we get another bottle?"

"Yes, we can. Let me go get it. I'll be right back."

Me and Debbie get to talking about our childhood and all the fun memories we had growing up when she gets a text. I'm not too sure about who the text is from, but whatever the text is about, it changed her mood immediately.

"Hold on, girl."

"Okay. Everything all right?"

"I'm not sure yet. I'll let you know. I gotta take this call outside."

Chapter 16

Black Male at His Finest

DEBBIE GETS UP, walks upstairs, and heads out the door to step outside and continue her conversation.

Debbie says, "What are you texting me this bullshit for?"

Steve replies, "I been wanting to talk about work…and us, but you been ignoring my calls."

"So you make threats and use my son to get to me. That's not cool at all, Steve."

"Well, Debbie, as long as you and him stay in these streets doing what y'all do, I'll always have a reason to be in contact with you about whatever."

"I'm with my sister Evelyn right now. She just got in town. We was having a good old time till you sent me this punk-ass text."

"So the Meyers girls are back together again, huh?"

"Not like that, fool. She's here trying to find her daughter. We just getting our nails done."

"I know why she here. Remember, I talked to your nephew Diamond the other day at the hospital, and he came to the station. He told me everything. I know that those boys jacked him up last week, and y'all was just retaliating. But why didn't you call me?"

"You have enough going on with all of the crime happening here in Cleveland. We ain't here waiting for you to find my family anyway. We have our own resources. So if we have any leads, we acting on 'em."

"Acting on 'em? I'm not calling you because y'all out here just trying to find your niece."

"So what are you calling me about then?"

"I'm trying to help us out here. It's how y'all trying to find her. It's not okay that his crew and your nephew is out here taking the law into their own hands because he can't find his sister? Tearing up clubs, creating riots, and causing chaos wherever they go?"

"You of all people should know to find my family! I think it's okay and necessary for them to do whatever the fuck they got to find her! Our reputation ain't no goddamn secret."

"Listen! We have three men in critical condition, beaten damn near half to death, and we got ten more people with minor injuries from that brawl. There are people who claim to have witnessed everything and everybody involved. Too much heat is coming down on me, on business. You know that ain't smart."

"Well, who are they? And what are you gonna do about it?"

"I got a videotape and a stack of files with names on my desk right now. DJ's name is one of them. So get his ass in check, or I'm gonna have to tell him the full range of this business he running."

"Do what you gotta do, Detective."

"It's like that? Okay then, but I gotta talk to you about—"

"Bye, Steve."

"But—"

Debbie immediately hangs up the phone, frustrated and annoyed. She walks back inside, shaking her head.

I'm sitting in my relaxation chair with Darlene and April joking, laughing, and comparing men in the Midwest versus men on the West Coast. We talking about the differences, their similarities, and all the drama they put us through dealing with the crazy asses. Debbie comes walking back in. April is finishing up on my French manicure on the first hand while I'm sipping on my drink, waiting to switch with the other hand.

"You all right, girl? You looked pissed when you looked at your phone and went outside."

99

"I'm good, just business. Some fool trying to get me off my game. I'm a take care of it, though."

"Good! 'Cause we still having a good time in here."

Darlene says, "Yes, we are. Here, Debbie, take this. Get relaxed again."

Darlene pours another glass of champagne and hands it to Debbie.

Darlene says, "Alisha, waiting on you to get started on your manicure."

Alisha replies, "Take your time, Ms. Debbie. Whenever you ready."

Debbie says, "I'll be ready in a minute, girl. Just let me go to the ladies' room first."

"Okay, I'm already set up, so just come have a seat when you come back out."

Debbie walks over to the chair where me and Darlene are sitting to check out how our designs are coming out.

"That's nice. Y'all looking good, girls!"

"You know it!"

"Yes!"

Debbie goes to the restroom briefly, comes back out, and sits in the chair beside me to start on her manicure with Alisha. She can't wait to join the conversation, openly sharing all her crazy stories about the men in her life, giving a different perspective from the unique lifestyle she's lived. We continued having our girl time, drinking more and more champagne, gossiping, laughing, and crying, listening to one another's experiences. While enjoying the moment and the relaxing mood of the spa, I look around and notice that this establishment is quite small and is limited in space. With the mindset to do her a favor for this favor, I immediately go into realtor's mode.

"So, Darlene."

"Yes."

"I love your place, the elegance, decor, the ambiance, and your service is very hospitable. You're busy like this on a Tuesday, booked to the tea, damn!

"Thank you. I appreciate that."

"From looking around, though, it seems like you could use more room in here because I did see a lot of money walk in and out of the door because you were at capacity. Have you ever thought about expanding and/or relocating?"

"I have. We are growing a lot faster than I thought, and we could use a bigger building, but I'm in a great location. I can't really create more space or afford anything else. The rent is affordable, and honestly, business couldn't be better."

"What if I told you I could find you something with more space, and your rent would be the same or less?"

"I would love that. Where? Around here? When do you think you can you make that happen?"

"It's not far from here at all. Even though I live in Arizona, I still keep track of properties for sale here in Ohio just because. I actually saw this one online on my way here today. The property I'm talking about is right around the corner on Fourth street. Let me make some phone calls to some of my people here, and I'll get back to you in a few days."

"That sounds great. Thank you. I'll gotta call my cousin to see how she feels about it."

Debbie says, "Your cousin, what is she, your financial adviser?"

Darlene replies, "Were business partners, so I like to let her know about all the decision I make when it comes to the business."

Debbie replies, "As much as I come here, I ain't ever seen her, and you never told me about her. I thought you owned this spa by yourself. She must be a silent partner."

Darlene says, "She is a silent partner actually. I handle the books, I handle the business, and we split the profits 65/35. She invested half of the funds for this shop so I could get started. But because I spend all the time here and do most of the work, we both came to an agreement that that kind of split would be fair. She likes spending time raising her daughter. My cousin don't really need the money. She's just helping me."

I say, "Okay, well, I'll get back to you as soon as possible. I should have all the information for you by tomorrow. We can go check it out sometime this week if you want to."

Darlene answers, "You got it like that?"

"I do have connection around the country, yes. It's just part of what I do."

Debbie says, "I told you, girl. My sister is cold-selling them properties. She even helped me get a few houses that I'm renting out for dirt cheap around the city. I even got one in Brecksville."

"I'll talk to her. I think it would be a good idea to expand. Our business is growing, so we could use more space for all of the new clients we're gaining."

"Sounds good to me."

We finish up at the spa around eight thirty, leaving Alicia and April a nice tip for hooking us up and working later than their regular time. Me and Darlene exchange information, and I assure her that I will be in touch. I get sis to take me to Walmart so I can get the personal items needed that I can't bring on the plane. We walk around the store. I got me a cart, she walking beside me just looking, I'm grabbing soap, deodorant, toilet paper, and a few other items and snacks. Debbie's phone rings, changing her mood again.

"This dude just won't give up."

"Who is it?"

"You remember Steven Jones from high school, don't you?"

"Yeah, I remember him. He and Emmanuel used to hang out all the time, and they played ball together. Diamond told me he a detective now. What's up with that? Didn't he have a thing for you?"

"He still does. Hold on, Eve. Hello [*frustrated*]!"

Steve answers, "We need to talk soon, like tonight?"

Debbie replies, "Why?"

"They wanna renegotiate."

"For what? I'm not sure if I want to right now. We're really trying to find my niece."

"And why do you think I'm calling? That's my job. I can help you find her and keep all of y'all out of trouble doing so."

"I got too much going on, and you know you and we can't be around each other like that. It's bad for business on so many levels, so I don't know."

"It don't ma…" *Pauses then recognizes.* "I can see you now. Love the hair too. Looking just as good as the last time I saw you. Tell Evelyn I said hey."

"What! How you know what my hair look like?"

Too busy ducked off trying to keep her conversation on the low, twenty feet down the aisle carrying a shopping basket full of items standing six foot seven, eight, nine one of 'em, towering over everyone in the store, walking in our direction, is Steve—or can I say now Detective Steven Jones. He still looks good, though, I see, neatly groomed, clean-cut, high yellow professional brotha. It's good to see him because I do have some questions about my daughter. What I'm really tripping on is why he is calling sis so much. Well, I really just need for her to tell me the details about it."

"Ahh, Debbie."

I try to get her to look up and notice the figure approaching us, but she's focusing on her phone call so much she has no idea he's standing right in her face.

"*Debbie!*"

She lifts her head and turns around and sees Steve standing in front of her, smiling, calling her name after turning off his phone.

Steve says, "Debbie?"

Debbie answers, "Yeah, *what!* Oh, hey! What you doing here?"

"I'm shopping like you. What you doing here?"

"Um-hmm, you see what I'm doing here."

"Why you looking at me like that? I swear I did not know that I was gon' see you. Hold up. Is that Evelyn? What's up, lady?"

Suspicious and still trying to figure out his angle with my sister, I act cordial anyway and respond in a friendly manner, just to break the monotony.

"Oh, hey how you doing, Steve?"

I smile and wave, then continue looking for more things to add to my cart.

Debbie says, "You sure you ain't stalking me? After earlier, you just so happen to be where I am. Seems funny to me."

"Naw, I just got off work, and I'm picking up a few things before I go home."

"Speaking of work, my son told me that he talked to you the other day. He says that you have some information about my ex-husband and my daughter's last whereabouts."

Steve says, "I do, and when I saw you two, I felt I should come over and tell you what I know so far. At first I thought your son was just another case until I got to the hospital and read his chart. I recognized who he was, and I felt obliged to help. Me and Handles was boy's man, shit damn near brothers back in the day. Once Diamond told me all that happened with his father, your daughter India, and the strip club incident, I personally went out of my way to find out more."

Debbie says, "What you find out?"

I say, "Yeah, that's what I want to know."

"I'm getting to that. Hold on, ladies. Well, after doing some of my own research and contacting my resources in Raleigh, I found out that he stopped teaching over a year ago because he was indicted on sexual assault charges."

Debbie says, "Uh, uh."

I remarked, "Accused of what? That man never had to rape nobody. Who was the bitch?"

"Yeah, she just so happened to be the dean of college's daughter. Some loose-ass white girl that lied so her racist daddy could fire Emmanuel. I even heard that she used your daughter by hanging around the house a lot to get to him. He was put on suspension without pay and couldn't teach anywhere else until the case was over. All charges were eventually dropped because of lack of evidence, but by that time, he was so stressed about it that he became an alcoholic, gradually drinking himself to death. I think he passed away some months ago from cirrhosis of the liver. Your daughter became MIA not too long after that, and from what I'm told, no one in North Carolina has heard from her since."

"I just can't believe he died that way. I never knew him to be a heavy drinker like that. Did he have a funeral? Why wasn't me or my son notified about anything?"

"Your daughter was his beneficiary, and she wanted to have him cremated. India attended prep school and was taking classes at the community college Emmanuel worked. When everything happened, she felt it was best to disenroll herself from school because it was just too much to deal with. She sold his car. She sold their house and got rid of all of their belongings. Wherever she is, she's financially secure."

"What is going on with that girl? Why hasn't she called any of us?"

Steve's phone starts ringing.

Steve says, "I gotta take this call. Give me a minute?"

He takes his phone conversation two aisles away. We wait just to find out if he knows anything else. About a minute goes by, he hangs up the phone and walks back over to us.

"I'm sorry, y'all. That was work. Debbie, bad news."

"Bad news? What you talking about?"

"That was one of my officers. He's a close friend of mine, so he called me because he knows I know you."

"Okay, so?"

"Well, he got your son DJ in the back of his cruiser in Shaker Heights. Damn, boy was smoking and had weed on him. I thought you said you was keeping him out of trouble?"

"Goddammit! I am. So now what?"

"I can take care of it. Don't worry about it."

"Okay, what's the catch?"

"We got problems that need to be handled ASAP. Meet me at the spot, we a—"

"You serious?"

"Very. Like I said, this is important."

"Okay, just let me drop my sister off first, unless you still wanna go hang out tonight, Eve?"

"Well, I kinda did, but naw, I'll check in my room and get some R&R for the night. Make sure Diamond is all right."

Debbie says, "You make sure my son get home."

"I will."

"I'll call you and let you know when I'm leaving. Let's go, sis."

"And I'll text you when DJ is good. You ladies have a good night."

"All right, bye."

As he walks away with a worried look in his eyes, I get a sense that something is not okay. I ask sis out of concern.

"Sis, what's going on?"

"I don't know, girl, but we about to find out."

Chapter 17

DJ's Dilemma

IN THE BACK of this muthafuckin' squad car mad as hell. Seems like this asshole is waiting for me. As soon as I turn the muthafuckin' corner on 116th and Buckeye, damn cop gets right behind me and just swoops on my ass.

Naw, let me be honest, I ain't gon' lie. I am bumping the shit out of my music down the street. Smoking that OG with the windows down this late in Shaker Heights, yeah, not good. It's just sometimes I 'on give a fuck when I'm riding, man, nigga get to zoning out and shit. I am on my way to get some Rally's for me and Nora, then here this guy comes fucking up my night. I had a good-ass day too, me and my ladies spent all day together. We went to breakfast, we went shopping, watched movies, you know, enjoying our family time. Put my lil girl to sleep after we got back home, rolled up a nice L for us, and had a couple shots of Henny as a nightcap. Buzz kicked in, then I got that feeling to give her this thug passion. Me my fine-ass goddess fucked so hard and fucked so long we ended up getting hungry again. I was feeling so good and relaxed after that. Man, you know I had to roll up another fat one for me before I went to get us some food. Dolo was out, so I was on my way to drop this package off to him 'cause bro needed some for the night. Glad it was only a little bit. Cop smells the weed soon as he walks up to the car, so I know he will search my shit as soon as he puts me in his cruiser. He ends up finding the last quarter ounce I have with me in the glove compartment, stashed in my first aid kit. My bad.

Officer Daniel Adams, he is an older black cop, so I am not really threatened at all by this stop. It actually maked me feel a lot more comfortable with all the shit they been doing to us out here. He just keeps searching through everything I have in my car though, hoping he finds more. *Wrong!* After about ten minutes, I reach my head out the window to see what's going on and what's taking him so long.

"Aye! You ain't gon' find nothing else, man. That's all I had."

"Yeah, that's what everybody say till I find something else."

"I hear you, but at this point, you just wasting time, bro. If I had more, believe me, I would have told you, or you would have found it by now."

"You just sit there and wait, DJ."

"What? You don't know me to be calling me that?"

"Yeah, I heard about you, Derek Jr. Most of us know you and your family business."

"Yeah, whatever."

He continues searching everywhere anyway, he looking up under seats, he looking through my spare tire in the trunk. This nigga even checks up under the hood, the fucking hood! Trying to see if I have some drugs in my engine or some shit, this nigga! I'm thinking he just being an asshole doing all this unnecessary searching until a gray unmarked Crown Vic pulls up. He looks in the car to talk to the guy in it, then he walks back over to the cruiser. He opens the door to let me out, then takes off my handcuffs.

"Man, you lucky somebody like you. Get out."

"So, what, you letting me go?"

"I ain't letting you go. He is."

He points over to the unmarked vehicle. Getting out the car is this tall cornball Detective Jones punk-ass dude walking over to us. Somebody I don't care to see right now, even if he calls himself helping me out. I have a license insurance for this weak charge. I'll be bailed out by the end night. Have my lawyers on speed dial for shit like this. I really don't like this dude anyway 'cause he always trying to get at moms. And he a try to do that shit in my face like it's okay 'cause my dad ain't around. Like him being a cop won't get his ass knocked out or sent somewhere. I know he got something to do with setting my Dad up too with his degenerate-ass lawyer friend. He gon' get his though. Cop or not, we owe this nigga.

Officer Adams waits until he gets close, then shakes his hand.

The officer says, "We good?"

"Yeah, man, we good. I got it from here. I owe you."

"Yes, you do. All right, dog. Have fun [*he turns to me*] and you—"

"What's up?"

"Keep the music down. You know people gotta work in the morning."

"Man, I know. My bad. I was feeling good, and that was my shit I was bumping. Gotta a little—"

"[*Interrupts*] Just keep that damn music down! Got the whole neighborhood shaking and shit. Y'all young kids today, boy."

He tosses me my keys, then gets in his car and pulls off, leaving me stuck here with Dick Jones to talk to.

I say, "So you letting me go again, huh?"

"Yeah, you can say that."

"What you think, you be doing me a favor or something?"

"Naw, I don't think that. I don't want nothing from you, young man. I'm just here to help you."

"How you here to help me? By doing this?"

"You ain't this lucky, and you damn sure ain't this careful. Just know that I got my ways of knowing what's going on and who's doing what in this city. I've known your family for years now, so I look out because I can, because I'm supposed to."

"You supposed to?"

"So you telling me you never thought about how much dirt you don't get caught with, with all the shit you do? Anybody else that live the life that you do the way you do would have been in prison by now."

"Prison, huh? The way that situation just went down, with your boy waiting on you after he cuffed me, seems like you set this shit up."

"Let me let you in on something, son. Everyone in my department knows that if any badge ever stops you, your sister, or your mother to give me a call before they do anything. You see, I know what you do, Junior. We all know what you do. Your dad got locked down. His business didn't. Who else would he appoint to run his very lucrative company? A close friend, his first son, and or his wife. In our line of work, that's easy math. You'll learn one day that the only thing that changes with this game is the pieces. People come, and people go."

"Yeah, I hear you, Detective. I hear you loud and clear. Sometimes, for many of us though, you work with the cards you're dealt. When you born in a lifestyle such as myself and gotta hand like I do, you gotta play that muthafucka till the game is over. So thanks for the words of encouragement, but we all gotta part to play."

"Yes, we do. Yes, we do, but you better start playing smarter. Sooner or later, you won't be so lucky to have me around to keep you out of shit."

"Like you did my dad, huh?"

"Excuse me?"

"You heard me, Detective! Nigga, I know you and your boy blackmailed my pops. I know the shit you do just to keep yo' name clean from the shit you do."

He looks at me and laughs like it don't even matter that I know.

"What you hear?"

"I heard enough. I know y'all into every crime everybody else in the streets is into. I know y'all shake muhfuckas down so they can stay in business. I even heard about the after-hour's joint y'all got in EC selling liquor, weed, and pussy out that, muhfucka.

He pauses for a moment, takes a step back, folds his arms, puts his left hand over his mouth, and leans on the car.

"Hmm? You heard some shit, huh? That's good you heard some things, but at the same time, you have no idea what's really going on, do you?

"Fuck you talking about man?"

"Well, what your mom's or yo' pops didn't want you to know and what we haven't told you yet, while you walking around here with a problem with me, is… I work for your dad and mother. And you, really."

"You what? Mannnn, get the fuck out a here with that."

"I bullshit you not. Back in the day, I played basketball with your uncle Emmanuel all while we was in school. During my junior year of high school, your dad moved right down the street from me. We got cool. He showed me everything he knew about the game. I was with it 'cause I needed money, so after high school, I hustled for him on the low to pay for and get through college. For three of my four years on campus, I was the man to see if you needed any drug. I had what you needed from weed to coke, crack, X, lean, speed, candy dipped in acid, anything! I had everything. All my work came from your pops. I mean, we—"

"[*Interrupts*] It's kind of hard for me to believe anything you telling me right now, honestly. Like I'm tripping cause what, then you become a cop? Then you arrest him after all the shit you did for him? I don't get what you saying, like what you talking about?"

"Hold on, hold on, now I know, and I understand how you feel, but let me finish what I was saying first so you can understand where I'm coming from. For your information, Junior, your father is the one that helped me become a detective for the business you're in charge of operating right now. You see, your dad was smart. He was organized, extremely generous, all that shit. But at the same time, he was aggressive, demanding, manipulative, and fucking crazy once he went there. He figured with having eyes and ears on what's going on in the department. We would always have the upper hand on our competitors and our clientele. We had a system inside the system, and the money was coming in fast and easy. In the beginning anyway. My position kept him safe and out of trouble the best way I could. But because your father was so reckless and hotheaded at times, he would always get arrested for everything else but what we were doing. Mostly speeding or assault for fucking some nigga up in public over money. Some dumb shit he could a had anybody do. That was that

Texas shit, though. He had to let you know he he that type of cat that will still put in work no matter what. Shit was dumb to me 'cause it caused too much attention."

"Yeah, that sound like Pop right there, man. I seen him do the shit growing up. So what the fuck happened then? Why my dad locked up and you out here if y'all was working together?"

"It was that shady-ass lawyer your dad had so much love and trust for. Great lawyer, but he was frivolous as fuck when it came to spending money. Tony was about five hundred thousand dollars in debt to the Carcetti family."

"Five hundred stacks? Damn! From what?"

"Being coked up all day and losing money gambling at the crap table and poker table every chance his dumb ass got. See, the mob not only wanted the money he owed them. They wanted a piece of our business too 'cause they knew he worked so close to us. Tony felt like he should have been getting more money than he was getting even though your dad was paying him like five to ten grand a week to keep everything under wraps. He also made money off his other clients, but representing the mob who was our biggest competitor kind of put us in a bad situation. He knew our revenue stream so his greedy ass found a way to help them out by paying off his debt and break up our operation."

"What happened?"

"At the time, I was head of the narcotics unit, keeping every-thing we did under control, which is why we never had any problems with any shipments being jacked, busted, or stolen. But because the mob has police chiefs, judges, and mayors on payroll, they found a way to get me transferred to the homicide unit. Your father on the other hand was busted by some Italian cops not too long after that. They made me come along so it could look like I set him up. Me and your pops knew what it was though. We never knew how Tony was planning to pay the Carcetti family back. All we know is that one day he just disappeared, and our business was disrupted."

"Damn, so you telling me that even with you being a cop, y'all can't or don't have no way of finding this dude nowhere?"

"As of now, no. Remember, this is some other business that I really can't have the department knowing I'm into. I do have some of my own resources on the lookout for him, so I'll know soon. Just give me a minute."

"All right, that's cool. So what is it you need me to do right now to help?"

"First thing is, after the other day and this situation tonight, we gon' need you to stay out the way for a while. We—you and me—don't need this kind of attention. Especially when we trying to find a way to get your pops out, all while still trying to find your cousin."

"A man, that's just how we do, man, them niggas touched family on top of stepping up while we was just trying to get some answers about lil cuz."

"Your moms is pissed too."

"My mom? A man, what's up with you and my mom? If you supposed to be working for me and my family, why it is that you always flirting with my mother? Disrespecting my dad and shit?"

"You want the truth?"

"Yeah, I want the truth 'cause honestly, I don't like that shit at all, man, for real."

I ain't gon' lie. I always had a thing for your mother, man. I was digging her way before her and your father dated. He got her. I started working for him, and I backed off, way off shit that brotha crazy. When he got locked up back in 2007, she called on me. She needed me, and I was there for her. I was the closest man around whom she could trust, real talk, man. Your dad knew about it."

"He knew about it! The fuck you mean he knew about that!"

"I tell you this, not many people, male or female, that can wait three to five years for somebody. She gon' have an itch that you can't scratch or do shit about. What do you think you can actually do about it from in a cell?"

"Man, I...fuck her ass up if she do anything with any mutha-fuckin' body."

"Really, DJ, so you can stand there and honestly say to me as a man that if she get locked up, you ain't gon' have sex with any other woman for three to five years? For real?"

I stands there and think for a moment, face scrunched up, trying to give my answer.

"Yeah, you don't even have to answer that. I already know what it is, young blood. You see, I tried to stay away and forget about it, you know, do my own thing. But your dad kept going back and forth to jail. Your mother kept calling me and calling me, and even though I didn't want to, I did, just for her. I'm in a confusing situation, but I'm good. We gotta keep the business going, get your dad out, and now find your cousin. You stay up on your end, and just like tonight, I'll hold up my end of the bargain with keeping you off these streets and out of jail like yo daddy."

"I got you, man. Good looking out too. Hit me up or whatever. I do gotta talk to my mom though 'cause that shit sound crazy, dog. I can go, right?"

"You got it, bro. Do your thing, and yes, call your mother."

"I will stay up."

Chapter 18

Good to Know… Finally

I'M POSTED UP, still hanging out over Brittany's spot, enjoying every bit of this beautiful woman's company. Cherishing every moment we have together before we part ways and I have to go back to school in Los Angeles. We ain't really did much else in the last few days but chill, talk, eat, and have sex, but that's the kind of relaxation I've been needing. It's Thursday evening. We sitting here watching movies and eating Chinese food. Going back and forth debating about one of the last movies we just watched.

"Ain't no way! That nigga Hulk will smash the fuck outa Thor in a fistfight. Hell, he can even bring his hammer. That shit won't even matter."

"I don't think so. That lighting, once he charged it up from the universe, Thor will burn Hulk's ass to pieces for real."

"Girl, you crazy. Hulk can take that weak shit."

"Nope."

"Yes, he can."

"Nope."

"Whatever, woman. Yes, he can."

We both take a moment to laugh about it, smile, and continue enjoying our food. I pause from eating for a minute, then get up and put in another movie.

"Hey, I'ma go check my mom out at the hotel when I go pick up some more clothes tomorrow. It a be around one or two in the afternoon. I wanted to know if you wanna come with me. Or do you think it's too soon to be meeting moms and thangs?"

"[*Sarcastically*] Yeah, I think it is too soon, Diamond."

"For real?"

"I'm joking with you. I'm cool with meeting your mother."

"Cool, I'm a call and let her know. We gotta meet up over my grandmother's house with DJ and my aunt to talk about finding India. I ain't really heard from nobody, so we gon' see what it is tomorrow."

"I know right. Well, just let me know. I'll come."

"Cool."

We finish the movie and our takeout, chop it up a little longer, then make our way back to her bedroom to end our night off full of passion. 9:43 a.m. the next morning, I wake up rejuvenated from last night's activities. I pick up the phone and call Mom immediately.

The phone rings.

"Hello."

"What's up, Ma? What you doing?"

"Nothing, just getting up. About to get me something to eat and get dressed. You still coming this way?"

"Yeah, that's why I'm calling you. I wanted to know when you wanted me to come out. I got some clothes to pick up while I'm there too."

"You can come by around two to two thirty like you said. You don't have to rush, though. I'm still getting it together. You talk to your cousin yet?

"Naw, why? What up?"

"Police had him pulled over with something on him the other day."

"Damn, for real! I was wondering why I ain't heard from him. I did text him yesterday to see what's up too."

"Well, I talked to Debbie 'cause it happened a few nights ago, and she told me that they let him off with a warning. I don't know how, but he end up going back home that night."

"That's good then, right?"

"I guess,"

"I ain't talk to him either 'cause we all been staying out the way since that situation at the bar. We should see him today over Grandma's house. He did tell me he would be through, but I don't know."

"You should keep his butt on the right path. But okay, Diamond, I'll be here when you decide to come up. I'm in room 908."

"That's cool. I'll be at you soon as I grab some stuff from my room. I'm a few doors down the hall in room 912."

"Okay, bye. Peace."

I hang up the phone with Mom, get dressed my damn self, and make my way out to see her. I get to the hotel about a quarter till two. Brittany actually follows me in her own car. Even though she can't stay, she still wants to meet Mom and see Auntie. She has some of her own things to do, then we gon' hook up later.

* * *

We enter the hotel lobby where I see Aunt Debbie, one of the most stylish, fashion-driven diva general managers in any hotel across the planet. I see her behind the front desk talking to one of her front desk agents when we walk in. So I get her attention.

"Hey, Aunt Debbie."

She turns around, sees me and who I'm with, then smiles in awe, watching me and Brittany. She steps around from the desk to come and give us both a hug.

"Aww, baby, you two do make a cute couple. How you doing, Diamond?"

"I'm good, Auntie. Just been hanging out with this young lady here."

"Hey, Brittany, come here with your beautiful brown self, girl. Nice to see you."

"Hey, how you doing? it's nice to see you again. Love your hair."

"Thank you, girl. You know I gotta stay sharp just to stay sharp."

"I see."

"Y'all looking for your mother?"

"Yes."

"Well, y'all gon' head up. I just talked to her a minute ago. She was getting ready."

"Okay, cool, we 'bout to head up. It's good seeing you again, Auntie, and thank you for everything. You coming over Grandma's with us?"

"Yeah, I'll be there soon as I get off."

We pass the front desk area, head to the elevator, and make our way to the ninth floor. I rush to my room, grab a few of the outfits and accessories I needed to stay at Brittany's again, then we walked out and headed to Mom's door.

Knock! Knock! Knock! Knock!

"Who is it?"

"Ma! It's me, Diamond!"

"Okay, hold on."

It takes her a few minutes to answer. She opens the door, sees me, and starts crying immediately. Although we both haven't seen India in a few years, me and Mom haven't seen much of each other in person in about a year either, being in college and her working so much. Making sure I'm okay and intact, she examines me, turning me all around to see if I had any marks or cuts anywhere. Looking at the slowly healing black eye and scratch on my face from the brawl at the bar my last few visits, she gasps, then pulls me close to give me one of the biggest hugs I think I have ever gotten from her. I quickly respond by embracing her and holding her as tight as she hugs me while Brittany stands there and watches in silence.

"Hey, Momma, I got someone I want you to meet. This is Brittany. The young lady who helped me find out about India's friend and her brothers. Brittany, this is my mother, Ms. Evelyn Meyers."

"Hello, Ms. Meyers."

She looks at Britt, smiles, and pulls her close to hug her as well in appreciation for her assistance and being in my favor.

"How you doing, sweetie? Thank you so much for everything you're doing to help us find my baby India. I really appreciate that."

"It is no problem. Once I heard about what was going on, I felt like I had to help in any way I could. Nora is my girl, actually family, and DJ and Faith, so I go all out for family."

"Yeah, Ma, Brittany has been a lot of help. I'm happy cuz introduced us. So what's up? I been to my room and grabbed what I needed already. You 'bout ready to go?"

"Yeah, I'm ready. Let me go and grab my purse, and we can leave."

We wait for her in the room while she gets the rest of her stuff, then stops by the front desk before we leave to see Aunt Debbie.

"Hey, sis, you talk to Momma today?"

"I did this morning. She said she was gon' be home all day cooking. I told her all of us was coming over today."

Mom wants to make sure she is home, so she stops for a minute to call her now, just in case.

"Girl, you know Momma be on the go these days now that Daddy ain't around no more, so let me call this woman"

The phone rings.

"Hello!"

"Hey, Momma, how you doing?"

"Hey, Evelyn, I'm in the kitchen cooking. When y'all coming?"

"That's why I was calling. We was about to come over there shortly. Just making sure you was gon' be home."

"You guys can come whenever y'all want to. I'll be here. Your sister Audrey called. We talked for a minute, and I told her what's going on with India. She said she might come tonight and take tomorrow off if that damn government job she got allow her to get some free time."

"Aww, that's cool. Wow, I ain't talked to sis in a minute. Is she okay being out there in Cincinnati by herself?"

"Yeah, she good. Just working keeping herself busy. She told me to tell you to call her when you can."

"Oh, okay, I will. You can give me the number when I get there. We on our way, Momma."

"Okay, Eve, I'm here."

Mom hangs up the phone and puts it in her purse; we say our goodbyes to Aunt Debbie, then head to the parking garage. While heading to our cars, Brittany says goodbye to Mom as I escort her over to her vehicle. We separate with a hug and kiss, also making arrangements to see each other again later. She gets in the car, pulls off, and we pull out right behind her, finally on our way to see my grandmother.

It's been a few years since the last time we all saw my Grandma Meyers together, so I know as soon as we see her, it's gonna be a lot to catch up on. I let Mom drive on the way there 'cause there are a few old spots from her yesteryears she wants to check out since she is back home and all. We pass by her high school, her first job, her old stomping grounds, and all the neighborhoods of people in East Cleveland her and dad used to know. When they separated back in the day, everything happened so fast we never got a chance to know about all the stuff they was into when they were younger. I can see in her face right now, she feeling some type of way.

"You all right, Ma?"

"Yeah, I'm good. Just thinking about your father and us back when…"

She pauses for a moment, takes her time to speak while holding in tears she's been trying to release since we see each other.

"I'm… I'm good, Diamond. It's just so much nostalgia and memories I have here. I grew up here. We just…we just got to find my baby India and put this broken family back together."

"Yeah, I know. I really do miss what we used to have when it was all of us—me, India, and you and Dad. I mean, you did a good job with us, but you know."

"We did have some great time raising you two. Shit, we had some good time together period until that…that…"

"That what?"

"Nothing."

"Come on, tell me. I never asked before, and I always wanted to know what really went on with you and Pops, Ma? For real? Was it that bad to leave as fast as you did? Breaking me and Dia up like that and now all of this?"

"I'm gonna be real with you, Diamond. Yes, it was that bad *[angry and emotional]*, and it was hard, very hard for me—a working, loving, committed, supportive, honest, sexy-ass black woman that's loving her black man—to be put in a position to even have to make that kind of decision. Break up my family! Change my entire life, only take one of my children because that black man I love is a great father even though he hurt me like hell."

"I hear you."

"Back then, you were older but really too young to understand what was going on."

"But you could have just forgave him and worked it out for family. I mean, that was Pops, though."

"Look, he was your father, a good man to his children, I get it. A good man to me most of our time together. You and your sister loved him and would have wanted us to work it out and stay together for the family. But it was not just what he did to me, us, Diamond. It was how he did it and what transpired from it."

"What did he do?"

"Do you remember the day he was supposed to pick you and your sister up from school, and you guys had to walk home, and you end up in the hospital?"

"I do. Damn, I was just thinking about that when I was in the hospital last week, okay."

"Well, that day after class, I was going to stop by his office and take him to lunch. I'm at his office door, and before I knock, I notice him and a student a little too close. I overhear their conversation about him leaving us and being with her as soon as he can find time."

"Na uhnn, I don't believe that, Ma. Dad wouldna done no shit like that."

"Diamond, I hear it and see it unnoticed with my own two eyes. I swear on both of you. I calm myself down, go work out, and I swear to you not I run into this bitch at the damn gym that same day."

"You talking about the bitch Dad fucking with?"

"Yes, some tall Italian skinny swimming bitch. I didn't realize while I'm trying to look at her and see her face from the mirror, she already know who I am. Got the nerve to say some slick shit to me in front of her friend about your father while I'm leaving. We get into it. I knocked her on her ass, really."

"For real, Ma, you whooped her?"

"Put it on her! Hell yeah, but right when I was about to dawg-walk this heffa, she tell me she pregnant by your father."

"What! Naw!"

"She end up calling him, telling him about what happen with our situation. He go tend to this girl and their baby not pick y'all up, and you end up in the damn hospital. So to answer your question again, *yes! It was that bad!* Got dammit!"

Diamond sits there shocked, stunned in silence by this new unwanted information he just received about his father, realizing the move.

"I loved your father with all of my heart for ten years, never cheated, lied, or hurt him. Some sacrifices must be made even if it hurts your soul doing it. I did that for us, not just for me."

"Damn, Dad was a bitch-ass nigga for that. Wow, so you heard about him and that chick in North Carolina then, right?"

"Yeah, I heard about it."

"With you telling me that I don't want to, but did he do that shit there with that dean's daughter? Shit, I don't know now."

"Me either, but that do sound kind of shaky. Your father never had to rape no woman with all the women that wanted him."

Driving down Van Aken, we make a right on to Shaker Heights and pull up to the house. DJ, Nora, and Faith is already here 'cause his BMW is pulled up in front of Grandma's.

"Looked like DJ here already."

"That's his car?"

"Yup, him and aunt Debbie, they on some other shit right now."

"I like that."

Me and Mom sit in the car for a little bit longer to finish our conversation.

"So wait, I have a brother or sister out there?"

"I guess y'all do, somewhere either here in Cleveland or some-where else. I don't know. You wanna find him or her?"

"What's crazy is, I do. Even though Dad hurt you, us, I would love to add somebody else to, well, we gotta find India first to be complete. Pops rest his soul."

"Yes, Emmanuel Diamond Williams, you rest your beautiful soul, king. We will put this family back together."

I get out the car first. Mom gets out, I walk around to her side of the car while she's getting out to give her a big hug and let her know I understand why. I tell her that I love her and how much I appreciate what she did for us. We finish up our moment and head up to the house.

Chapter 19

Reunited and It Feels So…

"Good to be home where it all started. I really do miss being back here. So many memories."

Walking up to the door, I can see Mom grinning as she looks around the yard, the house, and garage, blessed to have been raised in an environment and lifestyle for her parents to still have the same house she grew up in.

"Everything still looks the same since the last time I was here."

"Do it?"

"Yeah, it do, but you can tell Daddy ain't around no more to keep up with the landscaping."

"It don't look that bad."

"Naw, it don't, but not like Daddy would have it."

We step up on the porch and tap on the door to see the front door open and the screen door unlocked. So we just walk right on in.

"Hey, anybody home?"

"Yo! It's Diamond and Mom!"

Running out to come and greet us at the doorway is Faith's adorable self with a melting red popsicle in her hands.

"Hi, cousin Dime!"

"Hey, Faith, what you doing with that popsicle?"

"Eating it."

"Okay, don't make a mess."

"Oh my goodness, who is this little gorgeous lady we got here? Hiiiii!"

"Hi, I'm Faith. What's your name?"

"I'm your Auntie Evelyn. You can call me Auntie Eve."

"Hi, Eve."

"Are you gonna be okay with that?"

"Umm hmm."

While we standing at the entranceway talking to this little girl, the kitchen door swings open. Grandma Hope comes walking out smiling, sweating with a towel in hand and the aroma of home-style cooking following right behind her.

"Hey, there they go. Come here, baby. It's so good to see you again."

"Hey, Ma."

Mom turns around, stands up, and gives Grandma that warm and loving hug a mother and daughter have.

"It's so good to see you, Momma. How you been holding up?"

"It's been going, I'm hanging in there, Eve."

"Okay, now where that boy at? There he is. Come here, boy."

"Hey, Grandma, what's going on?"

I walk over to give her a great big hug.

"Done been in town a week and just now coming to see me."

"I've been meaning to, Grandma. I just got caught up with some stuff after the hospital. I been hanging with D a little bit—"

"[*Interrupts*] Yeah, I know. I heard you done got caught up in some girl, that's what it was. But it's okay. You here, and I see you now."

"Yes."

"You getting some height on you, ain't cha, boy? I see you on TV. Y'all did good this year. Gotta look up at cha. How tall are you now?"

"I'm 6'3", still growing though. I'm happy to see you."

"Yeah, it's good to see y'all again too."

"I smelled it when we got out the car. Mom told me that was probably you. What all you cooking?"

Rushing out the living room from watching the news, here comes DJ's ass, attempting to cut her off and announce everything on the menu.

DJ says, "Maaan, what up, Dime? Hey, Auntie Eve."

Mom says, "Hey, boy."

DJ remarks, "Cuz, she cooking everything. You gon' love it. She making what, Southern fried chicken. She grilled some beef ribs yesterday that's slamming, homemade mashed potatoes, macaroni and cheeeeese, collard annnnd mustard greens. Ah, ah...what else, Grandma? Ahhh."

Grandma Hope says, "I got some potato salad, coleslaw, pasta salad, fruit salad, I made banana pudding, cherry cheesecake, and some other stuff. Y'all can go check it out in there."

"Whaaaat? Yeah, let me please do. Ma, you coming?"

"Naw, you go in there get you something. Let me talk to Momma for a minute."

I walk over to DJ and give him a pound, then Nora walks out the living room carrying Faith's little bad butt.

DJ says, "What's up, baby?"

Lenora says, "This little girl done end up making a mess with that popsicle all over her outfit."

I say, "I knew it!"

DJ remarks, "It's all good. You packed another one, didn't you?"

Nora answers, "You know I did. I'm about to change her now."

"Aye, I want you to meet my auntie, Evelyn. This Diamond's mother."

Mom says, "How you doing?"

"Hey, nice to meet you."

"Nice to meet you. Congratulations on your engagement. I see it shining."

"Thank you."

"And go 'head on getting that degree too, girl. You keep representing for us sistas like you know how."

"You know I am, and thank you. I really appreciate that."

I say, "What up *(smiling and grinning)*?"

Nora answers, "Hey, boy! How come I ain't seen my girl in a couple of days? You come in town hook up with her and take up all her time."

"I have done no such thing. What you're talking about? Me and B have been hanging out, that's it."

"Umm hmm, you and B, huh. Y'all got nicknames for each other now. It's okay, though. I talked to her. I told her I'm gon' tell you I want my friend back."

"I can't make you no promises while I'm around, but I'll see what I can do?"

"You better."

"I got you. What up, cuz?"

DJ answers, "Ain't nothing what's going on. Yeah, man, after you get you a plate, come holla at me in the backyard. I wanna rap to you about some crazy stuff."

"What kind of crazy you talking, bad stuff?"

"Well, naw, not really bad or good. Just some stuff."

"Oh, all right, cool. I'll be out right after I get my food."

"That's what's up. I'm about to roll up. We ate when we got here. I'm just waiting for my mom so me and her can rap. That's the crazy shit I'm speaking."

"Huh? What you mean?"

"I'll tell you."

"All right."

I walk in the kitchen to make me a plate, DJ heads outside to do his thing, Nora takes Faith upstairs to wash her hands and clean up the popsicle she spilled over her dress. Momma and Granny go in the dining room to sit and talk at the table.

"Dang, Momma, you went all out with the food, didn't you? I would ask the occasion, but—"

"Yeah, girl, I ain't cooked like this in a while, especially with your daddy gone. I wanted to do something special for my girls and grandchildren while ya'll in town."

"Well, thank you. We definitely appreciate you doing all this for us. The food smells really good."

"Y'all eat up as much and take what y'all want."

"You know I am gon' have me in the gym all next week eating like this. Me and Deb's crazy self hung out the other day. We had a good time too. I was gon' call you when I got off the plane, but by the time we did our thing, it was late, and I was tired, so I just went back to the hotel."

"Yeah, she told me she was picking you up from the airport. Where y'all go?"

"We went to a friend of hers spot downtown on Lakeshore called Spa Marengo's. We got manicures, pedicures, facials, and massages. Getting the pampered treatment. Sis hooked it up and wouldn't let me pay for nothing."

"That's how she is, always gotta do it big. She making money, so just let her do her. Most I do is just tip now."

"I told her she ain't gotta worry about me asking no mo. She wanna spend, I will let her do her thing. It was good though and very much so needed. It helped me relax without overwhelming myself thinking about everything that brought me back here."

"You know I understand, baby."

"So, Momma?"

"Yeah."

"You ain't heard nothing about India so far? I mean, she ain't get in contact with none of y'all?"

"No."

"Diamond said she should be somewhere here in Cleveland. He found out about her friend, so…"

In a bit of a situation and desperate to avoid giving out any information too soon, Hope hesitates to reply.

"I been asking around and hoping yo sister, and some of her people in the streets would come up with something, but I ain't heard nothing yet, Evelyn. I believe she okay, though. That's probably why we ain't heard from her."

"I 'on know, Momma. Don't you think she would have at least called and told somebody something by now."

"Maybe. Or she just may not be ready to talk to us yet. Think about your baby sister. I just talked to her again the other day after being mad at me."

"Well, yeah, I get it. I just wish Diah would at least let us know she all right. How long has it been since you talked to Audrey, Momma?"

"Almost two years, right after your father's funeral. Like I said, it's in ya'll blood to be stubborn. Your sister, your son, and your daughter got it honest just like you did."

"No, not like me. I ain't stubborn. I'll tell you what it is, but stubborn not I."

"Not you, huh?"

"No."

Not you?"

"*No!* Why you keep asking me that?"

"Well, if you're not stubborn, then why did you just up and leave split your children up, then move across the country 'cause of a man, huh?"

Caught off guard by Momma's response, Mom chokes on her words and hesitates to answer herself.

"Because... I..."

"Because your husband cheated on you. Like I said, stubborn! You didn't think about the rest of your family. You were a grown woman who could make her own decisions, I get it, but with making that decision, did you think about how this could affect your children's lives?"

"I did. I just—"

"[*Interrupts*] Or did you just think about how it could help you get away from the pain that man left you? Me and your daddy wanted to be there for you and the kids. Hell your sister did too. But you and your stubbornness just left town, and we had to connect with our grandchildren in different locations and different times. And by the way, just in case you didn't know, that broke their poor little hearts. They resented both of you two for it too, and this they both told me."

"You right, Momma. You right. I didn't, I wasn't thinking. I just reacted without thinking about the kids. I was running away from my problems because I was too hurt to deal with them. I see now. I see now that all of those problems caught right back up with me. So if you can please, Momma, please help me fix this."

"I will. I sure will. And, baby, truth be told, you'll know soon that your momma got her own problems she gotta fix that I need you and your sisters help with."

"What do you mean?"

Continuing their conversation staring out the window watching traffic pass by, they see a gray Chevy Tahoe casually rolling down the street. It slowly pulls in Grandma's driveway. A male in the passenger seat and a female driving. Not too sure of who it is, right away, me and Momma get up, walk out the dining room, and step on to the porch to greet whoever this is. The women steps out the car.

"Hey, Momma. What's up, Evelyn?"

To our surprise, it's Audrey and a male friend of hers.

Grandma Hope says, "Heeeey, baby, I thought you wasn't coming over till tonight or tomorrow."

"I was, but I really wanted to see everybody, so I took some vacation time and booked an earlier flight right after I talked to you. I'll be here for a few days, then we headed to Montego Bay, Jamaica. No work for me for the next few weeks."

Audrey Alayna Meyers, my momma's beautiful little sister. She was darker than Debbie and Momma, always neat and professional. She had a slim but curvy figure with long straight hair. Quiet, intelligent, and about her business just like all of us. After college, she began her career as an information technology specialist in the department of the treasury for the IRS. Been there for some years now making good money. She singly owns her home and works most of the time, so she stacking her paper. That's why it is such a shock to see her here with a guy

Mom says, "Okay then. Hey, Drey, what's been going on with you, sis?"

"You know me, work and more work till now. I'm doing pretty good though. I see you looking good as usual. How's everything been going?"

"Girl, I'm hanging in there, still searching for my baby."

"And that's why we all here. To help find my niece. Hey, I want to introduce you guys to my boyfriend, Malcolm."

Car door opens, and the short well-built dark-skinned gentleman dressed in a fitted black tank top showing his physique and some Army fatigue cargo shorts steps out the car to greet us.

Malcolm says, "Hey, good afternoon, ladies."

"Hey."

"Hi."

"Malcolm, this is my mother, Hope, and my sister Evelyn. Mom, sis, this laid-back chocolate brotha right here and I have been dating for about six months. We've known each other for a couple of years through work, of course. He just asked me out one day, and we hit it off from there. He's one of our project managers."

Audrey shuts her door, walks up over to the steps to greet and embrace me and Momma with hugs. After grabbing a cooler of drinks they brought with them from out of the trunk, he walks over to the front porch, sits the cooler down, and introduces himself with a handshake.

"Audrey thought it would be cool to bring something to drink for us. Hey, how y'all doing?"

A conscious brotha, I see, and I say that by looking at his tattoos and wristbands, pro-black this and that. We used to seeing her with those prestigious educated guys. Real sadity acting men. Go 'head then, sis!

"We doing all right. How you doing? Nice arms."

"Thank you."

"So you dating my daughter, huh?"

"Yes, ma'am, I am."

"How are old are you, young man? You got kids?"

"I'm thirty-three years old, and no, I do not have any children yet, I say."

"Momma, don't get to grilling him like that now. We just got here. Baby, don't mind her."

"I don't mind at all. It's cool. She got every right to know who her daughter is dating. Audrey talks about you ladies all the time. It's really nice to finally get to meet you in person."

"Well, it's nice to meet you too, Malcolm. I know you been keeping my little sister safe in the Nati. Thank you for coming."

"Thank you for having me."

Audrey says, "Who in the house?"

Grandma Hope answers, "Derek Jr., his fiancée, and baby girl was in the living room. Diamond in the kitchen getting something to eat. All we waiting on now is Debbie."

"When she supposed to be here?"

"Any minute now. She texted me she on her way about forty-five minutes ago."

"Good! Come on, Malcolm. Let me introduce you to my nephews. My other niece is studying abroad in Africa somewhere. Come on."

Not too soon after speaking her name, here she comes, music bumping down the block with my younger cousin Dennis in the car this time, DJ's little brother. Right on time, yelling out the car.

"Hey, y'all, the queen is in the hooouuusssseee!"

Grandma says, "Well, queen, it took you long enough to arrive."

Aunt Debbie replies, "Momma, you know how that place get this time of the year, weddings, family reunions, polka. I had to help my new second-shift girl check some client in so they don't get backed up. What's up, ladies!"

Momma says, "Hey, Deb!"

Aunt Audrey says, "What's up, sis?"

Aunt Debbie remarks, "Long time no see, stranger. What's up? How you been? Say hi to your auntie, boy."

Dennis says, "Hi."

"Hey, baby boy. I'm doing all right. Girl, get yo' high-class butt out the car, girl. We a talk."

"Okay then, I got you. Come on, boy."

Chapter 20

Family Ties

AUNT DEBBIE, LIL cuz Dennis, Audrey, and her new boyfriend, Malcolm, all make their way inside to meet, greet, and get reacquainted. We all take the time to eat and put something on our stomach before we started making drinks, listening to music, and having a good time. Mom decides to start up a game of spades between the adults while Dennis and Faith play video games downstairs in the basement. Grandma is back and forth monitoring the kids and watching the card game when she can. Me and DJ go outside to smoke to do our thang. The teams playing spades are Malcolm and Audrey against Mom and Debbie. Crazy right.

Mom says, "It's on us to bid?"

Aunt Audrey answers, "Yup."

"All right, Debbie, how many you got?"

"I got about three and a possible."

"Okay. we going 7. It's on y'all."

Aunt Audrey says, "Baby what you got?"

Malcolm replies, "I got like 2"

"That's it?"

"Yeah, that's it."

Aunt Audrey says, "Okay, we a go 5."

Mom says, "5 okay, we up 22 to 18. It's on you, sir."

Malcolm says, "Cool."

Me and cuz watch 'em play their hand a little longer, then we head out in the back and sit on the patio to smoke and chop it up. He get to telling me about what's going on between Aunt Debbie and this Detective Jones cat. How he been working for the family business for all these years and how he trying to get Derek Sr. out of jail and all that. It does start making sense though 'cause when I went to the station that day after I got out the hospital, they didn't want to come up. And when I was in his office, he was asking me so many question aboutAauntie. I get it. So we smoking, talking shit, and he keeps filling me in on some other stuff when Nora comes walking outside and hands me the phone.

"Here."

I look at her and DJ for a minute in confusion, then, "It's Brittany."

"Oh okay. Hey, lady, what's up with chu?"

"Hey! What you doing?"

"Nothing, just sitting over my grandmother's, chilling with them. What, you coming through to see me?"

"I wanted to if it's cool with you? I just got off work, and I can hang with Nora while y'all do what y'all do."

"Naw, I don't mind at all. I want to see you anyway. Come on."

"Okay, let me talk back with Nora."

"All right, here you go."

"Me and Faith gon' go out on the front porch and wait for her."

"All right."

"Yup."

I hand the phone back to her, and she go in the house. Me and DJ keep smoking while we listen to Mom and nem old-school Luther Vandross jams ("Never Too Much") bumping inside. Sounds like they arguing again in there about something, probably the game.

Aunt Audrey says, "See, that's what I'm saying. Y'all keep underbidding!"

Aunt Debbie answers, "What you talking 'bout? We won with a jack of clubs and the last book. We ain't know we was gon' get them books. You just mad 'cause we set y'all ass."

"I ain't mad. You don't know how count your hand right, that's what it is! Cheating as usual just to win. You get on my nerve doing that. You did that when we was growing up. Didn't she, Eve?"

Mom says, "Uh oh, here we go again. I'm trying to relax, enjoy myself, and play cards, and these two got me stuck in the middle of another one of their disagreements. Every time we get together I gotta play the voice of reason. We ain't been around each other like this in over ten years, and still when we do, sooner or later, I have to calm the fire and ice women down at the same time over something.

"I'm staying out of this. I ain't saying nothing. Let me enjoy my buzz. Whose turn is it to deal anyway?"

Malcolm is sitting in his chair, looking real uncomfortable. Anxious to hurry up and play the next hand, he helps us out by changing the subject back about the game.

"I believe it's on me. I got it. Don't worry about it, Audi. We 'bout to come back on 'em. Let's get it!"

Out of nowhere, sis just blurts out, "I'm just tired of everybody in this family always doing shit behind my back and thinking it's okay!"

Mom says, "What?"

Aunt Debbie says, "Girl, we playing cards. It ain't that serious. You overreacting as usual. Get over it."

Audrey, our always quiet and always laid-back little sister who never really says anything mean or out of anger, all of a sudden, must be feeling something in her today to make her just lock up on Debbie.

"Get over it! Get over it! Look, Debbie, I know a lot more about what's going on around here than you do, so you need to stop acting all high and mighty. You have no idea. Momma and Daddy didn't give me permission to do what I wanted to do. They kept me in my books, made sure I stayed away from boys and fun while you did whatever. Hell, they didn't even tell me everything I had a right to know. Ain't that right, Momma?"

In comes Grandma from out the basement, sitting with the kids. She walks in curious and frantic, instantly asking questions about all the commotion going on with the crazy sisters.

"What you two in here arguing for now!"

"Yeah, her and daddy let you to be you, Dee. However, you wanted to live the lifestyle you live. They accepted the man you married, they accepted the money you make, and they accepted the way you make it. Sometimes you need to step off your high horse and stop thinking you're better than everyone at everything! Damn!"

Aunt Debbie says, "What are you saying, Audrey, and where is all this coming from? You know what I do. Shit I helped yo ass doing what I do. Everybody know what I do. I'm a businesswoman. Don't judge me on how I run my business."

"Yeah, crooked and illegal."

"What! Bitch, fuck you!"

"Fuck you!"

Malcolm says, "Hold up for a minute. Baby, I thought you were gonna do this differently? Baby, calm down. We just playing cards. You wanna go outside for a minute to cool off?"

"Naw, baby, I can't. Right now, me and my sisters and my mother need to talk! If you don't mind, can you give us a minute?"

"I can do that, ladies."

Malcolm respectfully gets up out of his seat, kisses Audrey on the cheek, then escorts himself to the kitchen.

Aunt Debbie says, "Momma, I don't know what got into your daughter, but you better calm her ass down 'cause I ain't the one. Ain't been in town a minute, and you over here disrespecting me like this. What the fuck is going on with you coming in here trying to front and check me 'cause your man here don't' get fucked up?"

Aunt Audrey says, "Yeah, I want to see that. You ain't gon' do nothing."

Mom says, "Audrey, baby, what's up? Why you coming at us like this?"

"Mom, you want to tell 'em?"

"Tell us what?"

Grandma Hope states, "Audrey, you wanna do this right now?"

"Yes, Momma, I do. I didn't come back not to. They need to know."

"Right now?"

"Yes, Momma, right now!"

Grandma Hope sighs. "Okay, let's talk."

"What's going on?"

"Look, Debbie, let me apologize to you first. I'm tripping, and I was out of line. I got into my feeling. I did not and should not have come at you like that. I was wrong. Ya'll know that's not me. Some things I know, and the past came out, and I'm so, so sorry. I really hope you can forgive me."

"You know I forgive you. It's cool, lil sis. You got out my hook up though, brought that bitch out girl. I was...whew!"

"I know how you get, and I realized it once you got up out your chair. I wasn't ready, had to check myself. I'm just upset and a little drunk, but—"

"Yeah, I'm buzzing too. You just lucky you my sister. We was about to have to take that shit outside, bitch."

"Shit, girl, I just did my hair. I ain't 'bout to be fighting with you."

"Me too, but I woulda did it anyway you need to know. Don't nobody talk to me like. But on the serious note, though, I do want you to know that no matter what I do or what I have done in my life, you should always know I would never ever, on Daddy and my children, try to cheat my family or friends out of anything. Anybody else, fuck 'em. I do live a different life, but with family, I don't play. You know I love you, Audi, and will always have your back, girl."

"I know you will. You always have. I'll always have your back too, sis. It's just my job now working for the government can be hectic and a little too personal at times. I really did feel like it was best for me to come back home to let some things out. What's crazy is that Malcolm suggested it. He's a good guy."

"I can tell. He seem like he had your back. We need 'em. Now come here, bitch, and give me a hug."

Mom says, "Awwwww, I knew ya'll better had to hug this out."

Debbie and Audrey walk around the table over to hug and forgive each other. Audi steps back and looks at Grandma.

Audrey calls, "Momma."

"Okay, okay. Debbie, Evelyn, y'all sit down for a minute."

"What's going on, Ma?"

"Yeah, what's up?"

"Well *[sighs]*, me and your father hasn't been completely honest with all of you over the years about some things. We knew we would have to tell you one day, but he got sick so fast we couldn't find the right time to. Right before he passed, we agreed that I would tell all of you myself once we all got together again. But because your sister here works for who she works for, searching through his records, she end up finding out before we could tell you two."

Mom says, "Okay, y'all gon' tell us, find out what?"

Aunt Audrey states, "Dad wasn't my real father."

"What?" Mom exclaims.

Aunt Debbie says, "Huh? He not what? Ma, what is she talking about?"

"It's true, you and Evelyn's father, Sherman Myers, my husband of forty years, is not your sister Audrey's biological father."

Aunt Debbie, *angry*, says, "So you saying that after all these years of chastising us about keeping secrets, always stressing about the integrity of being honest and you stand here today after thirty years and finally come out and tell us a secret that you and Daddy kept from us. That's some bullshit, Ma! Why?"

"Because of how you acting right now, Debbie! Okay! We was scared. We wasn't sure of how you guys would react. We didn't know if you two would start treating your sister different because of our mistakes, and we didn't want that."

Mom states, "We were all too close, Ma, to ever do something like that. We always fought, well, still do, but at the end of the day, we love each other."

Aunt Debbie says, "You damn right 'cause all I know is that we sisters and have been our whole life. Knowing all of this don't change the way I feel about my sister. Momma, I love you and Daddy, but I'm kinda pissed you just now telling us this. And what I really wanna know is what made you cheat on Daddy without protection."

Mom says, "Damn, Dee!"

"I'm just saying, though. Ma, you was out there being a little thot, Eww, Ma!"

Aunt Audrey snickers. "Girl, you crazy…stop!"

"Yo' daddy wasn't no angel either, so stop with your shade, lil girl."

Aunt Audrey says, "Ooop!"

"Sorry, Momma."

"Anyway, during that time, me and your father's marriage was going through a rough phase. We had a real hard time seeing eye to eye on a lot within the household and working and raising y'all or whatever. I had just had Eve, and financial obligations kind a kept us away from each other a lot, if you know what I mean. I suspected he was doing something after a while 'cause he spent a lot of time away from home, but I couldn't really prove it. Eventually, I found out from one of our close friends that your father and one of his female coworkers had they own little family on the other side of town."

Mom exclaims, "He what?"

"Yeah, he had another child, a son on me, on us. Your brother, Sherman Jr., was about three months when I found out."

Mom says, disgusted, "Damn, Daddy."

"Un uh!"

Aunt Audrey says, "Told y'all."

"Yeah, he had been stepping out on me, on us, for over a year with her. Her name was Pam Jones. They moved back to Detroit after he broke it off with her and came back home. He always sent money to his son, though. We made sure of that. I met him for the first time a few days after your father's funeral. He seemed like a nice young man. He works for Chrysler, I think, he told me. He told me he want to meet y'all if y'all would."

Mom says, "Maybe one day."

Aunt Debbie shakes her head. "Wow! I don't know what else to say."

"And because I was so hurt then, I honestly didn't want him to have all the fun. I didn't. I couldn't. So I connected with a friend I knew from high school who was home from the service. Morris Washington, Audrey's father, was someone I could trust to do my thing with and keep it between us. It's just karma, well, you know. When I told your father about what I knew about him and about what I did, he was caught up, and he was hurt at the same time, real hurt. He wanted to leave but couldn't really say anything because of his own infidelities. He didn't expect me to play the same game even though I did not get pregnant on purpose by another man. Your daddy's options were us or them, take or leave it. As you can see, he stayed with us, and we both agreed then to never cheat again. It was hard, but it worked out. We just didn't really know when or how to tell y'all. I know he's not here anymore, and I don't want you judging him or looking at your daddy in a bad way. So please forgive us both when I say that I'm sorry that you all had to find out so late like this. I'm so sorry."

Slouched in her chair with her head down and her hands attempting to cover the tears falling, she continues to express her feelings about it all.

"He wanted to tell y'all when y'all were teenagers, but I still felt a little guilty. I didn't want to be judged, so I told him no."

Mom is crying. "Ma, we wouldn't na judged you. You and Daddy raised us to be forgiving."

Aunt Audrey, crying, says, "Yeah, we knew you guys weren't perfect. We would love you anyway."

Aunt Debbie is also crying. "Come on, Momma, don't be crying. We forgive you and Daddy. I'm sorry. I'm not mad. I love all my family."

The sisters gather around Grandma in the dining room and embrace her with love and forgiveness. They assure her that everything is going to be okay.

Aunt Audrey states, "Y'all the only family I know, and that's all that matter to me. I love y'all."

DJ and I walk in the room from outside, still laughing from our outdoor smoke-out. Unaware of what's going on, we walk in on the ladies while they're all still huddled up, crying together. We both pause in mid-conversation, turn around, and walk back in to where they come from.

I say, "Heeeey, what's going on, ya'll?"

DJ says, "Aye ah, I think we should just head back. I don't think we should be in here right now, cousin. *[Whispers]* Mom, when you get a minute, come holla at me."

"Okay."

Nora peeks her head in the front screen door from sitting out on the front porch and calls for us to come out.

"Hey, DJ!"

"Yo!"

"Why don't y'all come out here with us. Tell Diamond Brittany just pulled up. And bring your daughter something to drink."

"All right, babe, I got you."

DJ rushes in the kitchen and grabs a juice drink for Faith and let me know I got company. Hearing that B is outside now, I hurry up and finish the bowl of banana pudding I made to snack on from the munches of smoking. Gotta head to the bathroom first, though, and clean myself up, make sure I'm good, check the breath, you know. I finish in there, then walk back through to check on Mom and grandma and them before going out. I see Auntie Audrey's boyfriend, Malcolm, sitting in the living room area watching TV, chilling by himself. I check on him real quick.

"Aye, what's up, man? You cool?"

"Yeah, I'm good, brotha. Thanks for asking. Y'all all right? Look like y'all feeling pretty good."

"Yeah, yeah. We straight, but ah, I, ah, hope everything was cool with us, you know, doing our thing and all. I heard you work for them folks too with Auntie."

"All man y'all good, don't trip. I used to get into that myself. I just had to stop for, you know, work reasons. But I don't hate on nobody else for doing they thing. I know you a good brotha. I seen you play too. I had y'all in my bracket last year going to the Elite 8. Your auntie brag about you all the time, bro. And I heard about what's going on too. We here to help any way we can."

"I feel that, and I appreciate you for even caring, man. That's cool. Yeah, you seem like a good dude for auntie. Thanks, man. You hear that?"

A phone starts ringing.

I ask, "That you?"

Malcolm answers, "Naw, that ain't me."

"Aye, somebody's phone ringing! It won't stop ringing!"

Aunt Debbie yells out the room, "WELL, ANSWER IT THEN."

"All right, I will! *[Mumbling]* Soon as I find that muhfucka."

Me and Malcolm look around to see where the ring is coming from, but we don't see it and can't find it anywhere in the living room. The phone continues even after going to voice mail, so I search around and follow the steady ring back into the kitchen. Looks like Grandma's phone.

"Candace Law? Who is that? Hello?"

Voice shaky and frantic, the young lady on the other end of the line desperately says, "Gran... Hella, hello... Whuu...whuu...?"

Breathing heavy and loud, I can barely understand what she is trying to say.

"Who is, who...who is this?"

"This Diamond. I'm Hope's grandson. Who is this?"

"Can I...whhuuu. Can I speak to her? It's an emergency!"

"I, ahh, think she busy. Hold on a second. You okay?"

"I'm fine. Can I talk to her?"

Not sure about who this is or what's going on, I walk in the dining room where the ladies are still talking to interrupt their conversation.

I say, "Aye, Grandma, it's for you. Some lady on the phone asking for you."

"Who is it?"

"She says it's an emergency. Candice, I think. That's what the ID say."

Oh shit! Let me see. Hold on a minute, y'all. I'll be back."

Grandma snatches the phone out my hand, pushes me to the side, then rushes out the dining room faster than I've ever seen her move.

I say, "What's up with that? Y'all all right in here?"

Mom answers, "We all right, just bonding, girl talk."

Aunt Debbie says, "Yeah, we chilling, nephew. We don't know what that was about though."

Chapter 21

Two in the Bush

AFTER A FEW minutes of talking to them and doing what I had to do in the house, I go outside on the front porch to see Ms. Brittany.

"Hey, what's up?"

Brittany replies, "Hi."

She greets me with a hug and a kiss on the lips this time right. She did it in front of DJ, Nora, and Faith, who was already out there cuddling up on the porch swing. All of us were shocked, but as they watched in awe, they couldn't help but say something

Nora says, "Ooohhhh, y'all go 'head then."

DJ says, "Okay. I see y'all, all caked up in shit. Brittany, don't be getting my cousin all sprang like that. Make him look soft."

I say, "Man, shut up. Ain't nobody sprang, and you know damn well I ain't soft."

Brittany says, "You better be sprung for me."

"Come on now, girl. You know I am. He don't need to know that though."

A couple of minute pass, then Aunt Audrey and Malcolm come out to sit and talk with us. Mom, Aunt Debbie, and Grandma stay in the house along with little Dennis, who never came from out the basement. We all doing our thing outside on this nice summer night till about 10:30 p.m. when, all of a sudden, we hear Grandma come running down the stairs, yelling to us.

Grandma Hope says, "Evelyn! Debbie! Everybody! Y'all get y'all stuff. We got to go. We gotta go right now!"

Offset by her urgent need to leave at this time of the night, we instantly panic, thinking it's something about her health. Audrey reacts immediately to stress her concerns on the matter.

"Damn, Ma, you okay? Something wrong? What's going on? Why we gotta leave?"

"I can't get into it right now, but I'm fine."

I stand up to go in and do whatever it is I have to do so we can leave. While getting myself together, I notice Granny putting food up, closing windows, and turning off the TVs. Confused and a little worried, I ask her the same thing.

"What's up, Nana? What happened?"

"You'll find out when we get there. I'm sorry I just can't say until then."

Now I'm really nervous and curious at the same time about what this Candice chick tells Granny to make her get all roweled up. I see Mom walking over to ask her something. Nana brushes her off and continues closing up the house for us to leave. She then pulls a large bag from out the closet to go with her.

Mom states, "Ma, everybody wanna know what's going on and why we leaving. And what do you got that for?"

"I need to bring this with us. I'm so sorry, baby."

"Sorry for what?"

She then turns and looks at me with sadness in her eyes, hesitant to tell me what it is.

"I'm so sorry both of you."

I ask, "What you mean?"

"We don't have time, and it's just too much to say, so y'all come on. I'll tell ya'll when we get there. Me and you Eve, we gon' ride with Debbie. Audrey, you and your friend can follow us. DJ, y'all coming too, and Diamond?"

She stops, then looks outside and notices someone different.

Grandma Hope asks, "Who's that out on my porch?"

"Oh, that's my friend, well, Nora's. I mean our friend Brittany."

"Oh she's cute little chocolate thing. With all that booty on her, I can see why she kept you from seeing your grandmamma."

"Yeah, she do got a lot [*cheesing*]. Stop it, Nana. But yeah, she came through to hang out with us. I'm cool with driving. She gon' ride with me. I can follow everybody. Where we going?"

Debbie appears from out the dining room with her purse in hand. Dennis trails right behind her with his head down into whatever game he gets on the tablet.

She says, "All right, I'm ready. Where we going?"

Aunt Audrey answers, "That's what everybody wanna know, but Momma won't tell us."

"Y'all just come on. We going to Twinsburg, so follow us. And y'all know with your sister Debbie driving, y'all better keep up."

"Twinsburg? Why??"

"I'll tell you in the car. Let's go. Let's go. Let's go!"

We lock up the house, pack everything and everyone up in cars, and take I-480 East to Twinsburg. For what, I don't know. Yet, anyway, but we on our way.

* * *

My mouth is dry from doing all this heavy breathing. I'm alone, hungry, sweaty and I'm dilating close to eight centimeters right now. A few more centimeters, and Dr. Boley will be on her way in to help me deliver little Emmanuel into this crazy world we live in. Can't wait, and I'm so excited to meet my little man. It's just me and the nurse in the OR. She's helping me as much as she can, but I realize at moments like these, I need family or someone close here with me. When I feel my water break, I call Delilah first and another close friend, but they don't answer. I leave them both messages. I know Nana will answer, but I also know everybody is at her house. I have to call anyway, can't help it. I need her right now; I need my family even though I know I'm gonna get bombarded with questions. I'm nervous as heck 'cause Nana is coming with everybody. Momma and Diamond too. Can't imagine what they've been through trying to find me. I know that one day I will have to face them. I just never thought it will be like this. I bet they don't even know they coming to see me. They better hurry up 'cause this boy feel like he on his way. Nine centimeters...

* * *

About ten minutes until we arrive in the 'burg. Sis is doing close to eighty miles an hour with the rest of them mobbing right behind us. She knows she better slow down once we get there. Troopers here have always known to be out, ready to pull you over. Mom is sitting in the back seat with Dennis, who finally fell asleep with his tablet in his hand, still playing. She's on her phone texting and ain't said a word since we left the house. We listening to 107.3 The Wave with smooth jazz playing on the radio, and the vibe is mellow in the car, but you can still feel the tension. I'm in the passenger's seat, anxious and annoyed. Patiently waiting a few more minutes to see if Debbie gon' say something about where we going, but she's as quiet as a mouse, just driving.

I say, "What's up, Debbie? You ain't got nothing to say?"

Debbie answers, "Naw, not really. I'm thinking. I just got some crazy news."

"Something other than what Momma just told us?"

"Yeah, I just talked to Derek. He say he may get out by the end of the year."

Mom Hope says, "How he gon' do that? He got busted with some shit. I thought he had to do all ten years this time? It's only been three."

Debbie says, "I don't know. That's just what he told me so. It got something to do with finding his lawyer or something. We a see, though."

I ask, "Momma, where we going? What's going on in Twinsburg?"

"Were headed to the Cleveland Clinic out here."

Debbie asks, "Why we going there?"

"To go and see someone."

I ask, "Who?"

146

"Well, ah...you all are gonna probably be pissed at me again. But after this, everything will work itself out and be fine."

"Uh oh, here we go again."

Debbie says, What's up now, Ma?"

"Over a year ago, I got a strange phone call from out of the blue."

"Okay," I say.

"It was a call from a young lady who needed my help, to help her friend. She told me that her friend had just lost a parent and didn't know what to do. The young lady on the phone was leaving college and coming back home here in Cleveland, Ohio. She wanted her friend to come back home with her, but she kept having a hard time getting her to wanna leave. Her friend couldn't stay where they were, but she didn't want to come home either."

I say, "Momma, I know you not talking about?"

Debbie says, "Wow! How did I not know? Ma, I see or talk to you every day, damn near—"

Mom *interrupts* her. "Listen, I'm not done! After all she had been through with her father down there, she did not, you hear me— *did not*—wanna talk to anybody, *anybody!* Her friend didn't know who else to contact that she knew, but my number was still in phone. So she called me. Before we got off the phone, I told her to have her friend call me. A few days later, she called again while she was with her and just gave her the phone. Shit, she refused at first. She really didn't want to talk to me either, but she eventually gave in and took the phone. I didn't ask her anything. She just talked. And we talked, and we talked till I was able to convince her to come back home to Ohio. But only on one condition, she said."

I say, "And what was that, Ma, 'cause I'm like... *[Exhausted]* I don't know?"

"She said that she would come home only if I don't tell nobody about her being back in town. And yes, not even you...or her brother."

"Why would she not want to talk to us though? I... I mean, last time we talked, she never made it seem like she had a problem or anything was wrong. I… *[Emotional]* I'm her mother. Why wouldn't she wanna talk to me? I'm her mother, not you!"

Mom is *crying*. "You think I don't know that? As a mother, you think I don't know how hard it is to not tell my daughter that I know where her daughter is? As a mother, with her being gone, I knew how you felt, but as her grandmother, I also knew how she felt. She told me if I said anything to any family and somebody tried to contact her that she would never talk to me again. I wanted her to trust me, so I promised her I wouldn't. She needed that and needs us. It just took her a little time it to be comfortable with it, understanding the value of family. She loved her daddy. I told you how she felt about you separating them. She couldn't talk to you and honestly still scared to, but now I think she's ready."

I say, "Okay, that's good. I think I'm ready to talk to her too. Tell my baby that I'm sorry and tell her everything. If her daddy ain't tell her by now. Me and Diamond already had that conversation recently."

Feeling every emotion Momma described earlier, finally learning India's whereabouts, and realizing why she's been missing, I am frustrated, happy, hurt, and relieved, just screams alerting everybody in the car and waking Dennis up out of his sleep.

"Aahhhhhhhhhh! Got! Dammit, Momma!"

Debbie says, "Girl, you all right? Calm down. Baby, go back to sleep. Your auntie just letting out some energy. It's all right."

"This shit is just crazy. We searching all over the place for this girl, Diamond leaving LA, going to North Carolina back here to Cleveland, get into some shit in the process, and she hiding somewhere in Twinsburg. Wow! What we going to the hospital for then? Is she sick? Did her asthma get worse? What's wrong with my baby?"

Debbie says, "I know ain't nobody fucking with her, is they?"

Mom says, "No, ain't nobody fucking with her, and she ain't sick, crazy asses. She's…well, she's waiting for us."

Debbie says, "What dat mean? She's waiting for us. Momma, you and these secrets, I'm, for real, they gotta stop. You got my emotions everywhere today. Finding out my sister got a different daddy, then I do, my niece who we been looking for all around the country right here in Twinsburg, and you knew all this time. Man, I tell you, you something else, Momma. You the one gangsta over here."

I say, "I know Diamond gon' be happy I'm about to call and tell him."

Mom Hope exclaims, "Naw, don't tell him yet. Let it be a surprise."

"Don't tell him? Well, can I text him it's a surprise then?"

"Yeah, go 'head."

"All right, I'm about to let him know."

I pull my phone out to text him. Diamond and Brittany are rolling as the tail of the group of cars now taking the OH-91 exit 37 toward Twinsburg/Hudson onto Darrow Road. His phone goes off in mid-conversation, talking to B about one of his college basketball stories. He waits till they stop at the light at the exit and looks at his phone.

"We got a surprise for you when we get here."

Diamond says, "She said they got a surprise for me when we get here. Wonder what she talking about?"

Diamond texts back, "What does that mean, a surprise?"

Brittany says, "Y'all hear anything from your sister yet?"

"Naw, not since that night at the club. I ain't check back up on it more 'cause I was waiting on my mother to get here. That's what's crazy too. I think they was talking about it earlier when they was together, but ain't nobody said nothing to me about her since we all been together."

Brittany says, "Yeah, that's crazy. You think she can be here?"

"I hope she is, but if she ain't, I'ma keep looking. I ain't come this far to stop now."

* * *

We get off the exit cruise down Darrow Road, then pull in the Cleveland Clinic Emergency Hospital parking lot four cars deep. We all get out the car and group up. Everybody slowly gets themselves together, still looking tired from the partying and drinking we did earlier. Nana grabs her phone, uses it, puts it away, then gathers us all together.

"Now I want y'all to know that you guys are the only family I have in my life right now. My husband of forty years, your father and grandfather, is no longer with us. Y'all are my everything, and I want to thank you for being here with me today. I feel free because a part of my past was haunting me, and now I can breathe. Nora, thank you for being a phenomenal young lady balancing school, work, and motherhood. Accepting DJ's hand in marriage and choosing to be part of the family makes me proud, giving me a beautiful little great-grandbaby."

Nora says, "Thank you, Nana. I'm happy to be part of the fam."

Grandma continues, "And, boy, you keep your butt out of trouble. You be the man you know how to be."

DJ says, "I will. I promise, Grandma."

"Audrey, I'm happy that we're back talking again."

"Me too, Momma, and I'm sorry for staying away for so long. I missed you guys."

"I missed you, and I love you, baby. I'll never do anything to hurt you again."

Aunt Audrey says, "I love you too. I know you didn't mean to."

"And, Malcolm…"

Malcolm says, "Yes, ma'am?"

"You take care of my daughter down in Cincinnati. It's good to meet you, and I appreciate you for bringing her back to me. Thank you."

"It was my pleasure. She does mean a lot to me, so I'll protect her with my life. Nice to meet everybody too."

"Debbie, you've been my rock since your father died. It wouldn't be much I would do without you. You hold it down."

Aunt Debbie says, "I owe it all to you and Daddy, Momma. Ya'll taught us well. You know I got yo back."

"I do, I do. Now, Diamond?"

I say, "Yeah?"

"You and your mother come with me."

She pulls us close to form a group hug, embracing us as tight as she can. We break apart with her standing between the two of us, grabbing both of our hands to escort us in. The rest of the group, Brittany, and all follow behind us as we walk inside. Nana gets the attention of the nurse's station and asks for direction.

Grandma says, "Candice Law?"

The nurse answers, "Law, okay, let me check. Yeah, she's in labor in delivery room 214."

Mom's eyes scrunches with a smirk on her looking at her momma with her head twisted to the side. Then she turns around and looks Debbie in the face.

Mom says, "Momma, no?"

"Yes, baby."

Mom is *excited*. "Momma, no! Ahhhhhh!"

Debbie screams, "Ahhhhhh!"

I say, "Grandma, what they tripping for?"

"Diamond, your sister is here. Your sister is Candice Law. She didn't want me to tell you, but she's been pregnant and wanted me to keep a secret until today. If your mother don't mind, I want you to come and meet your nephew first."

I stand there in shock for a minute. I walk away from everybody to have a moment to myself.

I ask, "She here, India, is here for real? And she okay after everything? Thank you, God. Thank you for looking out for my sister."

Grandma says, "You okay, baby?"

"I'm cool. I'm ready. Let's go."

Everybody else agrees to sit downstairs and wait till they can come up. Me, Nana, and Mom make our way to the elevator so we can go see India and her new little addition to the family. I've went through hell to find my sister and to make sure she is okay. I'll do it again if I have to. We get to the door, and I start getting butterflies like I do when I'm about to play ball in front of a large crowd or something.

Grandma asks, "You ready?"

Mom and I answer, "We ready."

Nana slowly opens the door, and we walk in.

"Hey, baby, look who I brought with me."

We open the door, and sis is lying in the bed, hair in a ponytail, looking exhausted with this small little bundle of joy in her arms. She smiles at us, then turns her attention back to Emmanuel, like he's the most important thing in the world. She notices us come in, and as soon as she makes eye contact with me, she just breaks down and starts to cry.

India says, "Oh, Momma, Diamond, I'm so sorry. I'm so sorry."

I say, "Hey, sis, it's cool. We okay now. We found you."

"Hi, India baby, you don't need to cry. We're just happy to see you. How you feeling?"

"I'm okay, I guess. It's been so long [*wipes tears off her face*]. I've just been waiting for him to get here to talk to you. Come meet your grandson, Emmanuel Diamond Williams. Dime, come meet your nephew."

"That's cool. You named him after Dad, sis. Look at little man. I like that you made his middle name after me too. I like that. Dang, he got a head full of hair. It's so good to see you."

India answers, "It's good to see you too, Dime."

"You look so much older than the last time we saw each other. To see you as a mother now, wow, that's crazy, sis. Well, you know we got you however you need us."

Mom says, "Yes, we do 'cause what's done is done. We can't change anything from our past. All we can do is work on today for tomorrow. You're my daughter, and all I care about is you being happy. Here, there, or anywhere."

Grandma says, "Amen to that."

I say, "Candice Jackson, you changed your name? And who is my nephew's father? What type of cat is he?"

"His name Sean, but honestly, I don't really want to get into all that right now. I just want to relax after this."

Grandma remarks, "Yeah, let her chill a lil bit. Y'all gotta lot of catching up to do, I know."

"That's cool. That's cool. I'll leave you alone, sis. Long as we don't have to fuck him up or nothing."

"No, you don't have to. He back in North Carolina anyway. Delilah told me about what you and DJ and his crew did to her brothers at her job last week."

"Shit, them nigga's almost fucked my career up. Cuz wanted to do more than that. They actually lucky. I wouldn't na called him if they didn't do what they did to me. I had to find you however I could. I was worried. school or nothing mattered until I knew you was okay."

"Yeah, I know. You gotta be big bro, and I appreciate you for being so overprotective. I want to let y'all know I do got somebody else coming to see me. I wanted you to meet her. We just got off the phone before y'all got here. She was the other person I talked to when I came back to town. I met her years ago with Dad. She's always been a good mentor to me when I needed advice."

Grandma says, "Oh, Delilah's on her way, baby."

India says, "Naw, it ain't Lilah, Nana. I think she said her cousin know Auntie Debbie. She's a silent partner to a shop or nail place or something she go to."

Mom says, "I think I know who you're talking about. Your aunt took me there after she picked me up from the airport. She gave me her card. Darlene."

"Yeah, that's her name."

"Yeah, she was real cool. She let us do our thing after the salon closed. It was real nice in there. They needed more space though, so I was talking to her about me possibly getting her a deal on a bigger building on the same side of town for just a little bit more cash per month. I can talk to her too and see if she's interested. What's her name?"

India says, "Here she come now. You can introduce yourself to her."

Grandma is holding baby Emmanuel, while Mom is standing by the hospital bed next to India.

I'm looking at the TV, listening to them talk. and soon in walks India's friend.

The friend, with an accent, says, "Knock knock. Hey, girl!"

India says, "Isabella, hey, girl, I want you to finally meet my mom and my brother."

I turn around see her and speak. Grandma, who's enjoying her time with her great-grandbaby, looks up to do the same thing. Mom, facing sis, turns around, looks at her, and just froze.

India says, "Mom, you okay?"

Mom says, "India, girl, what in…the…!"

To be continued…

About the Author

YAAQOV WAS BORN in Cleveland, Ohio, and grew up just a little over thirty miles south in Akron. A born lover and connoisseur of music and art, he has passion for writing that started through poetry. At twelve years old, he began writing lyrics to songs he and his family of musicians recorded and performed throughout the city.

Seeking a career in management at the University of Akron was too time-consuming for him to still pursue his dreams. After many years being a full-time employee, Yaaqov decided to become a full-time entrepreneur/writer/independent contractor with the government as a verbatim hearing recorder and basketball sports official. Yaaqov's interest and concepts as a writer are bold, honest, and relatable. *Broken Together* is his first novel. Yaaqov currently resides in Akron, Ohio, with his wife and nine-year-old stepson.

CPSIA information can be obtained
at www.ICGtesting.com
Printed in the USA
FSHW011027110321
79337FS